ADVENTURES IN PR

ADVENTURES IN PR

LEO PEARLSTEIN

ISBN: 1523734388
ISBN 13: 9781523734382
Library of Congress Control Number: 2016901845
CreateSpace Independent Publishing Platform
North Charleston, South Carolina

CONTENTS

ACKNOWLEDGEMENTS

I am dedicating this book to Helen, my loving late wife of 70 years who helped me start Lee & Associates Public Relations in 1950. She was involved in several of the adventures and helped us tremendously over the many years.

This book would not have been possible without the help of my support team. My two sons, Howard and Frank, who worked with me in the agency for over 40 years, participated in many of the adventures. They helped me find the proper photos and files describing these adventures. Howard also edited the entire book. My son, David, and his wife, Karen, helped me on the computer in the process of my telling the stories. Jessica Ikeda, a long-time employee, spent many hours transcribing and editing the original dictated story. Graphic designer, Bill Goldfine, created the cover and helped with the mechanics of the book.

My very grateful thanks to the team.

LEO PEARLSTEIN

When Leo Pearlstein founded Lee & Associates back in 1950, he had no idea he would one day be referred to as a "Legend of Food PR," as part of a feature in the Public Relations News publication, or be named a "PR superstar" in the Public Relations Quarterly magazine. TV Guide has even featured Leo and cited his ability and professionalism in getting his clients' products placed on television shows and in movies.

Over the years, Leo, who personally supervised all phases of the agency's operations and members of his highly respected firm, have won numerous awards for outstanding accomplishments in food industry public relations, marketing and merchandising from many organizations.

Pharmaceutical manufacturers, food conglomerates and major corporations have called on Leo's expertise in corporate communications. He pioneered in California agricultural commodity and generic promotions and has created and supervised successful programs for over 40 different food advisory boards, trade associations and co-ops, as well as state and federally-funded marketing groups. This includes industries such as almonds, apples, artichokes, asparagus, boysenberries, chives, corn, eggs, figs, grapefruit, papayas, peaches, pineapples, plums, prunes, seafood, tomatoes and turkeys.

Some of the commodity groups he has handled range from the Danish Dairy Board and the English Cheese Association to the Mexican shrimp industry. Beverage clients he has worked with range from Pepsico and the milk industry to Suntory International (a billion-dollar conglomerate which produces over a hundred whiskey, wine and soft drink products).

And because of his great knowledge of food, Leo was invited to participate in the first President's Council on Nutrition at the White House.

In this book, Leo shares some of his favorite adventures in Public Relations.

INTRODUCTION

Welcome to adventures in PR. These adventures started when I formed Lee & Associates, Public Relations in 1950 and went on for over 60 years, handling mostly food product promotions. My two sons, Howard and Frank, joined me in the 1970's, Howard with a degree in Public Relations from USC, where I received my degree in marketing many many years prior, and Frank with a degree in Mass Communications from California State University, Northridge. They are involved in many of the following stories.

Before I get started, let me tell you exactly what I'm talking about. This does not involve the day-to-day routine work in Public Relations, where you plan, budget, research, implement and reach out to the media on behalf of your clients. My stories are about adventures that happened as a result of opportunities.

There were two types of opportunities. If something happened in the press, pertaining to the subject that we were promoting, we would see if we could react with positive information that would be complimentary to our client. There were also opportunities that we could create by working with someone else, and including their product information with our messages. We call them "tie-ins." We would share costs for media and production or we would include their product in our recipes and they would include our product in theirs. We would both benefit with increased exposure without additional costs.

Some adventures occurred as a result of emergencies or mishaps, over which we had no control or that could have been prevented, if in the planning stage, there was no assumption that everything was perfect, which meant double-checking all parts of the upcoming program.

My first adventure was with Abbott and Costello and The Golden Egg.

I'm sure you will enjoy reading these entertaining stories and perhaps get some ideas that could be helpful to you in some of your activities.

Chapter 1

ABBOTT AND COSTELLO

Comedians Bud Abbott and Lou Costello were two of the most highly paid actors in the motion picture industry as well as radio, television and theater, too. In fact, years ago, they were the highest box office attraction in the 1950s. Their most famous routine was "Who's on 1st?"

Abbott and Costello were making a movie and we were reading the Daily Variety and the Hollywood Reporter and saw a small paragraph, which said "Abbott and Costello to coproduce a movie with Warner Brothers, 'Jack and the Beanstalk' ". Now what has that got to do with us? Well, one of our clients happened to be the California egg industry. Our job was to get people to eat more eggs. Now what about the movie "Jack and the Beanstalk?" Well, we remembered that in the early days - in our grammar school days – there was a goose that laid a Golden Egg in the story. Well the more you can talk about eggs, the more exposure you can get. And wouldn't that be great to have some movie stars that are so powerful and popular get involved with eggs?

So, we contacted Warner Brothers. After several days of going through channels we found Abbott and Costello's manager. And, after all, since they were coproducing the movie, they were not only getting a very high salary, but they were going to get the profits of the movie, in addition. We said we represent the California egg industry - all the egg producers in California - and we have ways of reaching so many people through our channels that the movie industry has not been exposed to. The movie industry has been exposed to the Variety, the Reporter, the scandals and movie entertainment; we've been exposed to the food editors all over the country, plus, radio and television food shows, and the big giant grocery industry.

It occurred to us that if we could get Abbott and Costello to be photographed with eggs and doing something with eggs and they could talk about their movie with the goose and the Golden Egg, that would be great for us. We could expose it and we could get all sorts of PR. Meantime we knew we had to do something for them. So we said, if we could do some recipes and send it out with photos of Abbott and Costello cooking eggs or eating eggs, we would get some good publicity. Believe it or not, they became very excited about it and said "Great!"

Bud Abbott and Lou Costello help promote eggs.

So after many discussions, we came up with several ideas that would be beneficial to both of us. For example, at that time was the beginning of putting coupons in egg cartons. Now you know how valuable coupons are. You read the Sunday paper and you see everybody getting coupons so they can go save money in the markets. Well, the egg industry, at that time, started putting promotional coupons in the egg cartons. So, we told Abbott and Costello's manager if he wanted to give us some messages about their movie, then they could print a little leaflet the size of a coupon that would fit in an egg carton. You could have the front side talking about the movie and you could show photos of Abbott and Costello, with eggs, of course; and then we could take the back side and talk about nutrition, taste and recipes. We could get these into millions and millions of egg cartons! In order to start the ball rolling, we made arrangements to take pictures of Abbott and Costello.

Egg carton insert – we sold eggs by the dozen, they sold movie tickets by the million.

In 1952, we came up with the promotional program "Two eggs for you in '52." Why two eggs? We wanted people to be sure they had two eggs for breakfast instead of one, for better nutrition. Here we are: we can say Abbott and Costello are too good eggs and we can talk about eggs and the Golden Egg. So that's what started the whole promotion.

We obtained a giant frying pan 10 feet in diameter. We had it sent to Warner Brothers studio and we had the studio's chef make a lot of eggs and put them in the frying pan, and have photos taken of Abbott and Costello next to it. We sent these photos to the grocery industry magazines to let the food industry know what we were doing. In our news release, we were letting the industry know they had these famous movie stars helping to promote our eggs. So, they should feature eggs and promote with us. Meantime, the publicity department at Warner Brothers sent the same photos and started getting exposure for our eggs and their movie in the entertainment press around the country.

Special 10-foot frying pan helped draw extra attention to our egg promotion.

You do not make a movie overnight. I learned from the movie industry that you trickle out the publicity, a little at a time. You make short releases and you keep sending out new information and that is what they and we did. They kept sending out all sorts of funny things about Abbott and Costello and eggs.

The publicist at Warner Brothers came up with a great idea. He said, "Why don't we go to Lloyd's of London and insure the Golden Egg for a million dollars?" We figured we needed a special egg for the publicity, and as luck would have it, there was an egg producer in Utah who was so impressed with our publicity that he got in touch with us and told us that he had a golden egg. Come on now, that is kind of silly isn't it? No. He said it was a golden egg. So we said, "Send it to us." He delivered this golden egg and it was not actually gold. But it was not white and it was not brown. It was sort of in between. We are not farmers. We are city folks. We did not know what to do. It was a real egg.

So we went to the University of California at Riverside, where they had an agricultural department. We contacted the department director and told him we have got this interesting egg. We want to know if it was real and how come it has got this almost yellowish color. He sprayed the shell and did different things to it. He said, it was a real egg and only two things could have happened: either the chicken had an infection or the feed caused it to change color. So we figured, we've got a very expensive egg and we could use that for publicity.

Believe it or not, Lloyd's of London wrote a policy. So that gave us another photo opportunity. Now the egg producer was so impressed and so excited that he got in touch with us again and he said he wanted a thousand dollars for the egg. Well, we already took our photos;

there was nothing else to do with it and we just didn't want to pay him a thousand dollars, so we sent the egg back to him and thanked him. Meanwhile he got a lot of publicity himself.

During this period, we found a little golden egg. It was not a real egg. It was actually a gold-plated cigarette lighter. It had two parts to it like the old Zippo lighters. You turn the top off and you have a cigarette lighter. But, if you don't know it, it's a "golden egg." From then on, we used it for publicity photos.

As even more luck would have it, it just so happens that part of our job was to get publicity for the annual convention of the Pacific Dairy & Poultry Association. That's a very important trade industry meeting with buyers from all over the country, as well as food service industry and the retail industry. The Secretary of Agriculture was going to be the keynote speaker and the governor of Utah was there, as well. The Secretary was a Democrat, the governor was a Republican. So it was politically correct; they were both going to be keynote speakers at the convention.

So we had enough nerve - I think it took nerve - to go to Abbott and Costello and say, "Listen, we're having this convention. It's not too far from LA. If you can come to our convention, we will give you an honor. It'll be national; we'll have the Secretary of Agriculture give you an award for drawing attention to good nutrition and we'll take photos, and you are two Good Eggs." Believe it or not - it happened to be on a Saturday - and they said "Okay, we can go. "

Can you imagine that, getting the two highest paid actors coming to your convention? So we sent out more publicity to the trade press, not to the consumers. Then, something crazy happened. The members of the egg industry were so excited about seeing movie stars that the attendance at the exhibit almost doubled. Twice as many people were coming with their wives so they could see the movie stars that were going to come on Saturday, and they could say, "We've got two of the biggest movie stars talking about eggs."

Friday, the day before the convention, was the biggest rainstorm in Los Angeles in the last hundred years. It rained and rained and rained. Everything was flooded. The buses couldn't come in, the trains couldn't move, the studio got flooded, schools were even closed, all the day before our convention.

So obviously, Saturday was going to be extremely inconvenient.

We went down to the convention on Friday and had trouble getting there ourselves. I got a phone call from Abbott and Costello's manager and he said, "I've got bad news for you. Abbott and Costello cannot attend the convention. We don't want to get stuck in the rain, we don't want to have them catch a cold, we've got a shooting schedule," etc.

Here I am, a 30-year-old young Public Relations guy and I have to get up in front of 3,000 people at a convention and tell them that the people they came to see are not going to be there. I got up to the podium and said, "Ladies and gentlemen, due to Mother Nature, I'm very sorry to tell you Abbott and Costello, our guests, cannot be here at the convention."

The largest egg producer in California was so mad that he threatened to fire me for making false statements about having someone show up at the convention. We got over that because there were enough other smart members that figured, we still have a lot of publicity going on.

We took our giant frying pan and we had the chef of the Coronado Hotel fry up around 40 sunnyside up eggs and used a big giant spatula to put them into the huge pan. Now incidentally, the Del Coronado is a wooden hotel. It's ancient and famous. The fire marshal would not allow any use of their fire in the grand ballroom, so it was a fake out. We had the eggs cooked in the kitchen and the chef brought the eggs out to put them in the pan. Now, there was a lot of television because they came to see the Secretary of Agriculture, the Governor of Utah, and they came also to see Abbott and Costello. But instead of that, we had the Governor and the Secretary flipping eggs in front of the cameras and we talked about "Jack and the Beanstalk" and the Golden Egg.

Utah Governor Lee (l.) and U.S. Secretary of Agriculture
Brannan flip eggs for the TV and newspaper cameras.

Well, everything worked out okay. It was tough. It was a great convention. Remember it all started from that little paragraph in the Variety and the Reporter. That was our first great adventure in Public Relations.

Chapter 2

SOME CELEBRITIES ARE GOOD EGGS

After we had such excitement with the Abbott and Costello promotion, we saw the great results, and decided we should continue this approach with other celebrities in the movies, television and sports, exposing eggs and good nutrition. It was a good idea so, we started looking for sources.

First of all, we contacted many of the publicity agents that work for the celebrities and told them that we were anxious to promote eggs and that we can reciprocate and do publicity for them, too. We started attending and volunteering at various charity events where celebrities would meet, such as the Jerry Lewis Telethon, celebrity tennis and red carpet events. The actors would meet there and perform and raise money for the charity. We would contribute our hard-boiled eggs as snacks.

Our spokesperson, Karen Lindsay, was nicely-dressed with a sash that said "Miss California Egg." They would mingle and wait to perform and they were hungry, too, so we were part of the volunteer group to feed them. In the meantime, there were loads and loads of photographers shooting for many newspapers and we had our own photographer, too. If we had a celebrity that was available, we'd say, "Would you like to take a photo with Miss California Egg? By the way, you're really doing a great job for the charity. How about if we made you a "good egg," and we'll make a presentation of our little golden egg and we can send a story out, write a caption that says, "You're good egg, and that you've done great things for our community?" They loved it.

In the meantime, we had acquired a supply of these attractive, little, golden eggs. They would be perfect for our goodwill, publicity program.

This is a chance for various celebrities to show that they were part of the community and as a bonus for them to get some positive publicity. We took loads of photos with well-known celebrities at various events. They were nice people and we got to send the photos out with stories and their publicity agents did the same thing and sent it to the entertainment media. As our account grew, this good egg program went on for over 20 years. We had a bonus, too. Because in the marketing business, you can do all the promotion in the world, but if you don't have the cooperation of the retailers and shoppers can't find the product they can't buy, they can't buy as much. So we had to encourage the retailers to make big displays of eggs and to feature eggs on special. Every time we had photos of celebrities with eggs, we would send them to the grocery trade publications, saying that celebrities are helping promote eggs. The grocers liked it, too. They saw the photos and it was one complete circle of promotion and merchandising.

Joseph Campanella, Karen Lindsey

Richard Harris

Karen Lindsey, Wayne Rodgers

Cesar Romero

Karen Lindsey, George Foreman

Wayne Newton, Karen Lindsey

It worked tremendously and again, this whole adventure, which went on for a long time, started with a little story that we were able to read in the Hollywood trade journals about Abbott and Costello. Here is another adventure in Public Relations that was really successful.

Chapter 3

DINAH LOVES OMELETS

Dinah Shore was one of the most popular television personalities in the country. She was an award-winning singer who was also known for her popular TV shows, including "Dinah!," "Dinah's Place," and "Dinah and Friends." Everybody loved Dinah. She was the Ellen DeGeneres of the 60's and set the pace for future female talk show hosts.

She also wrote several cookbooks including, "Someone's in the Kitchen with Dinah" and "The Dinah Shore Cookbook." We were always interested in anybody who wrote cookbooks because we wanted to see if they used any of our products. In one of her cookbooks, Dinah included a recipe that used eggs with chives, two of our clients.

So we contacted her publicity agent. We told him that she had mentioned our clients' products in her cookbook and that we would like to give her an award to get some extra publicity for everyone. It was our Golden Egg Award. It would help promote her cookbook and both of our clients' products.

We then made arrangements to take a photo of Dinah with the mayor of Beverly Hills. He also happened to be an egg distributor and was also the chairman of the California Egg Board. We photographed him presenting Dinah with our "golden egg." We sent the photo with a release to the press all over the country, giving Dinah and our egg client a good amount of publicity.

Dinah Shore, "America's Sweetheart," receiving the "Good Egg Award"
from Dean Olson, Chairman of the California Egg Council.

When we noticed she said she loved omelets in the cookbook, that gave us a new idea. Our friend Howard Helmer, who represented the

American Egg Board, was the world's fastest omelet maker. He was actually written up in the Guinness Book of Records. He cooked 427 omelets in a half hour. He also did demonstrations on TV and taught cooking classes showing how you can make an omelet in less than one minute. He was an outstanding showman and a really funny guy.

So, as part of our creating an opportunity, we decided that since Dinah wanted to promote her book, and since she had the TV show, we contacted her producer. We told him about our idea to have Howard appear on her show and teach her and her celebrity guests how to make omelets. We would do all of the preparation and bring all of the ingredients and props. He loved the idea.

He chose a date when he had lined up a great group of celebrities together, including Jimmy Stewart and his wife, singers Steve and Eydie Gorme and the great Lucille Ball with her producer husband. Wow! What a line up.

Howard Helmer (far l.), shows (l. to r.) James Stewart, Steve Laurence, Dinah, Edie Gorme and Lucille Ball, the fine art of omelet-making.

Imagine, Jimmy Stewart, who was really a funny guy, flipping his omelet and having it going all over the place, as well as Steve, Eydie and Lucille Ball having fun with theirs, too. They laughed, they kidded around and they competed with each other to see who could make the best omelet and how many ingredients could they put into it.

Dinah, who was a nutrition fan, stated, "Folks, this is really not only tasty, it's good for you, too." This was a fantastic segment! It was so good that it went on for nearly 20 minutes. It was actually longer than the original allotted time.

Everybody was pleased. And, of course, our egg industry client got exposure on 90 CBS TV stations around the country. We couldn't have paid a million bucks for publicity like that if we tried.

There you go. A little entry in a cookbook that mentioned "Dinah loves omelets," and that became a super, super, super adventure.

Chapter 4

ANYTIME IS TURKEY TIME

In addition to promoting the California Egg Industry, we represented the California Turkey growers. They wanted us to promote turkeys for other occasions, including Easter, Mother's Day and summertime entertaining – not just for Thanksgiving.

We started contacting the media with year 'round turkey recipes and were seeking opportunities to keep turkey in the mind of the retailers and consumers. We created a theme, "Anytime is turkey time."

It occurred to us, why couldn't we do the same thing with turkeys that we did with eggs? After all, as we all know, people go crazy over celebrities. They are interested in what they eat, what they drink, what they wear, what they drive and so on. If they were seen with turkey, they could certainly make an impression on the consumers and the retailers. So, we started pursuing that idea.

We contacted celebrities or their publicity agents and told them that we represented the turkey industry. We suggested that we could take photos of the celebrities cooking a turkey in their home kitchen or another site. We would supply a turkey for them to cook and would release the photos with stories about their upcoming movie or TV show and their favorite turkey meals.

In addition, we offered to include a photo and a favorite recipe of theirs in a weekly publication for which we supplied recipes called, "TV Movie Fanfare." This publication was distributed in over 10,000 supermarkets, which had over a million readers. We ended up with the most popular actors, sports and music industry figures. In addition, we sent photos and stories to food editors and grocery trade publications to keep turkey in the news the year 'round. Some food editors wrote complete features about the celebrities and their families enjoying the food they prepared.

This adventure went on for several years. Turkey became more popular during the year, of course, and still remains the most important entrée for Thanksgiving.

Leo Pearlstein, Liberace

Rita Moreno

Howard Pearlstein, Mickey Rooney

Andy Griffith

Buddy Hackett

Shirley McLaine

Chapter 5

SEXY JAYNE MANSFIELD LOVES TURKEY

Here is an adventure that was not only successful from a marketing point of view, but it was a fun and exciting adventure, too.

Sexy actress, Jayne Mansfield, was an up-and-coming Marilyn Monroe, back in the 60s. She was not only beautiful, but was smart, as well. And, she loved publicity. She was often seen in newspapers and magazines and on television.

In our activities for the turkey promotion, "Anytime is Turkey Time," we were looking for an attractive person to grab some attention by wearing an apron we created saying, "How about a turkey BBQ?" She was a perfect choice. At that time, she was appearing in a 20th Century Fox motion picture called "Will Success Spoil Rock Hunter?" We contacted the studio publicity director and suggested that if we photographed Jayne wearing the apron with a barbequed turkey, we could both benefit from tremendous exposure from the press. He loved the idea and had us contact her manager for approval. He asked us to pay for her services and that she had just recently received $3500 for cutting a ribbon at a new supermarket opening, a lot of money back then. We told him that we did not have a budget for that and that we would pay for the photography and the mass distribution of the release. Here is where the fun started.

Jayne posing in our Bar B-Q apron.

As a matter of principle, he insisted on some compensation. After much discussion, we agreed to give her a year's supply of turkeys to be delivered to her home, as needed. We ended up agreeing to 24 turkeys for her and four for her parents in Dallas, Texas.

We set up a photo session at her beautiful Beverly Hills home. During the year, her housekeeper would call us when she needed turkeys for a big entertainment party she would be throwing. I had the great pleasure of delivering the turkeys personally.

Between 20ᵗʰ Century Fox releasing the photo to a large list of entertainment editors and our releasing to newspaper food editors around the country, we received tremendous exposure. There was even a greater result that helped solve a big problem we had. The meat managers at the supermarkets were not too enthusiastic about our promotion and did not react to the "Anytime is Turkey Time" theme. They were still thinking of only Thanksgiving and were not featuring turkeys during the rest of the year. This was a challenge for us. But, Jayne Mansfield saved the day.

Jayne presents the finished turkey

We sent the photo of Jayne barbequing a turkey to all the national grocery trade publications and we sent photos to all of the major supermarke meat managers in the state of California and, practically every one of them put her picture up on the wall in their offices, which reminded them of turkey everyday. We were told by several of the turkey processors that this photo resulted in an increase by the retailers in featuring and selling turkeys. In the meantime, we kept delivering the turkeys to Jayne and ran out before the end of the year.

We had another bonus. It just so happened, there was a story in the press that Jayne Mansfield was to marry muscle man Mickey Hargitay, known as "Mr. Universe." It was a big deal in show business. So we decided to deliver an additional turkey to her and wrote a little note that said, "Dear Jayne, Congratulations and best wishes on your marriage."

The wedding was covered by all the major press including, radio, television, newspapers and magazines, like a Kardashian event these days. The West Coast Editor of Life Magazine asked Jayne, "Now that you're married, are you going to be a homemaker?" She said, "Yes." He added, "Are you going to cook for Mickey and your guests?" "I certainly will," she answered. "I love to cook." "What's your favorite meal to cook?" asked the editor. "I love barbecued turkey."

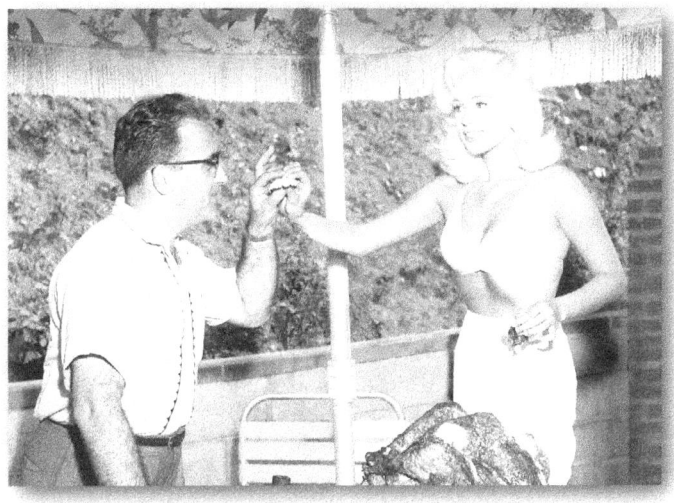

Leo promoting that "Anytime Is Turkey Time" – especially with Jayne Mansfield.

Wow! Can you imagine that? That hit the press all over the country. "Jayne Mansfield loves barbecued turkey." Imagine all of that publicity in Life Magazine. It was a publicity bonanza.

It was a great and quite successful adventure. It was fun and exciting and we certainly were pleased to have taken advantage of that opportunity.

Chapter 6

KENNEDY'S ASSASSINATION KILLS THANKSGIVING PROMOTION

This adventure, without a doubt, was the saddest that ever happened to us. It was devastating.

Every year, before Thanksgiving, we would promote turkey with Mrs. Cubbison's stuffing mix. Practically every TV station had a food show. We would arrange to have a chef or home economist appear doing demos on how to prepare the stuffing and show the viewers how to cook a stress-less and tasty turkey dinner.

One day, close to Thanksgiving, we had one spokesperson appear in Los Angeles on Channel 11 and another on Channel 13, along with all the ingredients, plus a cooked turkey to serve to the crew, after the show ended. I was at Channel 13, helping to set up the table and getting ready to start our cooking segment on the show when, all of a sudden a loud news announcement came on saying that President Kennedy had just been shot. Of course, we had to stop everything.

Can you imagine the shock in the studio? No one knew what to do! There was complete bedlam. Every station in the country spent the rest of the day and the next few weeks totally involved with this terrible story. We had spent weeks booking radio and TV shows, preparing menus and serving suggestions plus gathering props and making table arrangements. All of the radio and TV shows that we arranged for were cancelled. It was a very sad time for all of us.

Another problem occurred when it was the annual "President and turkey" photo shoot day. Every year, the National Turkey Federation would arrange for one of the turkey-producing states to send a live turkey to be "pardoned" by the President for the photo shoot. That year it was California's turn and we arranged to provide the live turkey. Photos were taken in advance and the photo prints were to be released just before Thanksgiving. We had the photos and releases ready, but with the announcement of the assassination we naturally decided not to send them out.

President Kennedy being presented with his special
Thanksgiving turkey that fateful year, 1963.

50 years later, Time magazine, had a cover showing all of the Presidents with turkeys and included the photo with President Kennedy. This is a perfect example of how an unexpected occurrence of which you have no control over can affect your promotion.

Chapter 7

STEVE ALLEN, FIRST TONIGHT SHOW HOST, A MAN FOR ALL SEASONS

This adventure was what I would call the most fun we could ever have, and yet, it was most productive and successful. Once again, it started with one item and went on for years.

Steve Allen was, without a doubt, in my opinion, the top television host. He was very gracious, very bright, very funny, and, he was the world's fastest adlibber. I can't say enough about him. He was just fantastic. He was the nighttime talk show leader way before Johnny Carson and Jay Leno and all of the other nighttime hosts. They all learned from him. He had many guests, celebrities and interesting people plus, he also performed, played the piano and sang. Besides being a tremendously talented person, he was also a health enthusiast. Many times he mentioned that he and his wife, Jayne Meadows, ate foods that were nutritious and good for you. What a wonderful opportunity for us. All of our products were in that category.

One time, we met with his producers and suggested that our many client spokespersons, such as Miss Prune, Miss Turkey, Miss Chive, and Miss Cranberry, would all make a great and entertaining guest. They were young actresses who were very attractive and bright. We gave them all of the information about the foods we wanted to promote, including delicious samples of the product for Steve to taste. The producers gave us an opportunity to present a guest and to see the reaction by Steve and the audience.

Steve cuts up while "Miss California Turkey" (Eve Bruce) soes the carving.

Steve learns about cooking with tasty prunes

Steve and "Miss Chives" (Carolyn Devore) clown around with her crown.

"Miss California Turkey" shares information and a lot of laughs with Steve Allen.

Helen Funai showing Steve the unusual Suntory bottle.

"Miss National Cranberry" (Karen Parker) pouring a "Steverino Smash" for its namesake.

We started with Miss Turkey who came on the stage leading a very large turkey. She started talking and told Steve that "Anytime is turkey time." We arranged for the prop man to bring out a cooked turkey. Immediately, they started having fun kidding around about the turkeys, live and cooked. To show you how fast an adliber Steve was, let me tell you about the first incident. The turkey made a deposit on the floor and the cameraman froze the camera to that spot. The audience howled and Steve asked her, "how much does the turkey weigh?" She said, "60 pounds," and he said, "More or less?"

There was a lot of fun and talk while Steve was carving the turkey. He said that he and Jayne, "love turkey all year long and that it was not only delicious but very good for you too, as it was high in protein and low in fat." Steve had the prop man bring in plates and utensils and serve turkey to his other guests calling it an all turkey show. Fun and discussions followed.

It certainly was an entertaining show and we were welcomed back for several years.

During the shows, both Steve the 'misses' tasted the food and said kind words about our products that included apples, chives, eggs, plums peanuts, boysenberries, and many more. That was an adventure that expanded from one to many.

Chapter 8

MRS. CUBBISON, A 60-YEAR ADVENTURE

Here's an adventure that began as a result of a small newspaper ad and from that, I got an account that lasted over 60 years.

I saw a two-inch ad in the Los Angeles Times that showed a package of Mrs. Cubbison's All Purpose Ready-To-Use Dressing, that had a picture of a stuffed turkey on the package, with a headline that said, "Turkey tastes better when stuffed with Mrs. Cubbison's Dressing." Well, that was certainly interesting to us and helpful to our turkey promotion.

An early Mrs. Cubbison's ad (greatly enlarged).

I tracked down Mrs. Cubbison at her bakery and found her to be a most charming and friendly person. If you like history of California Business Pioneers, I suggest that you Google "Sophie Cubbison" and you'll find a tremendously interesting story. It tells about her as a young teenager cooking for her father's 40 ranch hands before going off to college, where she majored in Home Economics. After graduation, Sophie Hutching married Harry Cubbison, and they became business entrepreneurs by starting a small bakery. In a few years, their company grew and it became famous for Melba Toast. Years later, she developed a popular dressing recipe using certain spices and broken pieces from the Melba Toast. This is how her famous Melba Toast dressing was developed.

I told Sophie that we were promoting turkeys and she certainly was helping our program and we'd like to work with her because we could both benefit from our activities, where her stuffing was promoted and our turkeys were promoted. She pointed out that she had a very small budget. So, I recommended that she could get more attention with a good food publicity program that I could develop. She agreed and hired us. That was the beginning of a very pleasant business and personal relationship and a successful marketing program for over 60 years.

Mrs. Sophie Cubbison, a formidable person and businesswoman, taught America a better way to make stuffing in the early 1950s.

We discovered early that Sophie would make an excellent spokesperson for her product and took advantage of her personality and her cooking expertise. We had her develop many simple, yet elegant, recipes using her stuffing mix and released them to hundreds of food editors. The recipes were very well received and drew a good deal of attention to her product. We made arrangements for her to appear on radio and television food shows. She gave cooking demonstrations and talked about how to prepare many different dishes, some of them included her product. This was not presented as an advertisement, but as an entertaining and educational cooking presentation. We even had her appear on some kid shows, such as Sheriff John, Bozo the Clown, Chucko the Clown and several others. She talked to the kids about food history and nutrition, on a level they could understand and we knew that the kids' mothers' often watch the shows with them, so they could learn all about Mrs. Cubbison's stuffing mix.

She was quickly becoming a "food celebrity." We also had her appear and do cooking demos at many state fairs. We also arranged for her to be a guest and demonstrate her cooking expertise at the various local gas and electric utility companies. We even had her participate at various events presented by the Home Economists in Business organization.

Sophie, who had worked all of her life, finally decided to do some travelling. She visited many places throughout Europe, South America and Asia, learning as much as she could about the various cuisines. She would send us letters and postcards with recipes from those areas. She would always be sure to be home for Thanksgiving. While home, she would visit all the various markets in her neighborhood to make sure her stuffing product was properly displayed. She would often call us and tell us that a certain market did not have a proper display and we would tell her company's management to send a salesperson to correct it.

After several years, Rold Gold Foods, which manufactured pretzels, offered to buy the company. She did something that is rarely done in business. She told them she would only sell her business, providing that they would agree to retain my company, Lee & Associates, as their advertising and promotion agency. They agreed and our "adventure," as described above continued. As the company grew, they added a variety of crouton products and our budget increased. There were several mergers after that and we still managed to remain as the agency of record until our 62nd year of promoting the Mrs. Cubbison line of products, when a new company, that had their own in-house promotion department, let us go. I believe that it was some kind of a record for an agency to promote a product for that many years and this adventure began all because of a two-inch newspaper ad.

Chapter 9

SAN FRANCISCO EXAMINER, NEGATIVE INTO POSITIVE

Herb Caen was a very popular newspaper columnist. His column in the San Francisco Examiner was called "Bagdad-by-the-Bay." He had many loyal followers and they would quote him and talk about his subjects at the water cooler at work. I remember reading his column the day after Christmas, one year, and his headline read "Let's talk turkey." He started off by saying "I hate turkey." His comments about turkey included everything you can imagine that was bad. For example, "people don't like turkey." "Turkeys are stupid." "They have too many feathers." "They look terrible." "They look worse when they're dead." He continued they were either too big or too small, too dry or too moist, that the neck took forever to take out of the turkey and all sorts of crazy little things. He said as many things that he could think of. Not only that, but he also said, that his friends didn't like turkey either, but they didn't talk about it. He said his friends would say okay I'll have turkey once or twice a year and have a couple of sandwiches, but there was no enthusiasm whatsoever. A lot of it was tongue-in-cheek and funny, but it certainly wasn't funny to the turkey growers, turkey lovers, chefs and foodies.

Herb Caen
— Baghdad-by-the-Bay —

Mumbling to Myself:

NOW THAT the big Eating Holidays are over, 'd like to say a few words about the turkey.

To use as few words as possible, I hate turkey. Everybody else I know hates turkey, too, but they're sneaky about it. Instead of coming right out and admitting it, they use such evasions as "Well, it's okay once or twice a year" or "Makes good sandwiches a couple of days later."

Or they don't say anything until you're about to carve them a slice. Then they smile weakly: "Not too much. A little of the dark will do nicely, thank you."

* * *

AFTER EVERY ated, you bring on t quite a sight, if it doe into the dining roo smelling horribly of t

The hypocrites and say "Ah." At le say "Ah." Then the more hypocritical tha veritable picture, tha carving, you can dis distant uncle withou thrust of the knife, bu His demise mere

There was an immediate reaction. We had phone calls from our turkey clients demanding that we do something immediately, such as demand a retraction, sue the newspaper and ask clients to cancel their advertising. We immediately got together with the manager of the turkey board and our partner in San Francisco and, we decided to use "honey" instead of "vinegar" and try to use humor in his style to communicate with him and his editors.

We had a lucky break. We had recently worked with the leading chefs from the finest hotels in San Francisco and we knew they would have been upset with the column. After several phone calls, we had six famous chefs roast a turkey and visit Herb Caen, and with a friendly approach, tell him perhaps "his" turkey wasn't cooked properly. We had the Chairman of the California Turkey Board, a leading turkey producer in California, travel to San Francisco and have him offer a "rebuttal" and point out all the positive things about turkeys.

January 1, 1954

Herb Caen Eats Turkey . . . . and Likes It!

As Johnny Mercer, the famous song-writer once said, "You've got to accentuate the positive and eliminate the negative." This action resulted in a fantastic article and photo that took up almost a full page. The headline read, "Herb Caen hates Turkey." Under the photo of the six chefs with their turkey, it said, "To his taste – columnist Herb Caen takes back the derogatory words he printed in his column about roast turkey." After many positive comments about turkeys he said, "It's great." A separate article said, "Fowl critic discovers his tirade was wrong." "Columnist admits 'It's good.'" And then, it continued with many more complimentary descriptions of turkey.

December 31, 1953

Herb Caen
Baghdad-by-the-Bay

Ring Out the Old:

COMES THE RESOLUTIONS: In 1954, I will not jaywalk—unless I'm in a hurry to get to the other side of the street and there aren't any cops around. . . . I will stop calling Artie Samish Smartie Samish; he's more Artie than Smartie. . . . I will not park in a bus zone while it is occupied by a bus. . . . When a waiter brings me a meringue glace when I clearly ordered a marron glace, I will blame it on my bad French and not on the good waiter. . . . I will stop needling cab drivers, because they're human, too; it's only the cabs that get out of hand. . . . I will never again make a left turn on a "No Left Turn" sign without giving a hand signal first. . . . And, as I dig myself out from under the letters and telegrams from turkey-lovers and Caen-haters, I hereby resolve to give the Great American Bird another chance; if the Caen-haters will do the same for me.

* * *

That was a great adventure and it confirmed our theory that there are ways of combating bad news by approaching it with positive information instead of anger.

Chapter 10

PRUNES AND JEANS

Who would have thought there would be a connection between prunes and jeans? We read a feature story in Advertising Age, the leading advertising industry trade journal, about Sedgefield Jeans launching a new advertising campaign to draw attention to the fact that their jeans were "wrinkle free." Their headline theme was "Eat prunes, don't wear them." We represented the California prune industry. Can you imagine our excitement? Here was a major advertising campaign telling people to eat prunes.

150,000 leaflets, many with winning
numbers, were given out to consumers.

We immediately contacted them and learned that they had a complete promotional campaign, including magazines and television and even a merchandising program. It included a kick-off in the massive retail clothing trade show called M.A.G.I.C., for all the department stores, where retailers and allied businesses attended to learn all about the latest fashions and programs dealing with clothing. We told them that we could tie-in and do promotion on our side, as well.

Together, we came up with a very exciting PR campaign. They added buttons, T-shirts, leaflets and contests for both retailers and consumers. Their prizes included a year's supply of prunes. Our prizes included jeans for the winners.

35,000 large badges were distributed to the prune faithful.

The T-shirt that became ten-thousand walking billboards.

10,000 bumper stickers gave our promotion even more exposure.

We sent humorous releases both to the general press and the grocery trade, drawing attention to this unique combination. We provided them with many sample bags of prunes to be distributed at the convention and even to hundreds of people shopping in stores for jeans with large Sedgefield retail displays. "Miss Prune" was at the M.A.G.I.C. exhibit and, for the next few months, we both created a great deal of attention to this crazy promotion about "no wrinkle" jeans and prunes. Since this was a strange combination about food and clothing, the news media reacted very positively and spread the word, "Check out Sedgefield 'wrinkle-free' jeans. If you want wrinkles, eat some prunes."

This program was a perfect tie-in. We both benefited with an unexpected increase in sales, plus positive attention and, because of its uniqueness, it turned out to be a fun and profitable adventure.

Chapter 11

PRUNES FOR ACNE

This adventure had many twists and turns. We were handling the Public Relations activities for the California Prune Advisory Board and at one of their monthly meetings, we were presented with a tremendous challenge.

When it came to the topic of "new business," one of the most influential prune growers took the microphone and told the group that his wife's doctor told her that eating prunes could help cure acne and that the Board should include that in their advertising and Public Relations activities. Everyone in the meeting was shocked, but did not respond because of his powerful position in the industry.

The California Department of Agriculture representative told the people in the meeting that they could not make medical claims in advertising. If it was mentioned, they would still have to have research to authenticate it. The Board manager told us to research this claim and report our findings at the next meeting.

That started an interesting series of events dealing with the medical profession. I first contacted a physician friend and he said that it was ridiculous (as we all thought it was). Acne is a disease of the oil glands and there are no known foods that cause it, nor do they know of any foods that cure it. Doctors recommend medication to help dry the acne. Just to have something official, I went to the dermatology departments of USC and UCLA and their reaction was the same.

I returned to the next meeting and reported all my research and, of course, the powerful member was extremely upset. In order to not offend him and recognize his suggestion, the Board discussed that perhaps we could do more research on the subject and come up with some new medical findings. They approved a $10,000 budget for "medical research" and gave us the assignment. With limited funds, we went to the University of California Davis, an agricultural University that works with the State Department of Agriculture and learned from them that prunes were high in potassium and low in sodium. Here were two positive aspects of prunes.

I went back to my physician friend and he told me that when he finished his training all of the medical students received a book explaining the benefits of foods and medicine. He had a list of foods high in potassium, listing oranges, bananas and others, but not prunes. That became our mission.

We also discovered, in talking to the Director of Pharmacology at Cedars Sinai Medical Center, that they had a problem with potassium medications that were too powerful for many patients, which caused ulcers. He suggested that it would be reasonable to promote aggressively, to the medical profession, that it would be wise to recommend prunes to the many patients that were taking high blood pressure medication to eliminate fluids. For the next year, we contacted medical associations (such as for heart, lung and cancer), various government agencies, hospitals and doctors. We sent the research material that indicated prunes were the number one food high in potassium and low in sodium. We even participated in the American Heart Association convention with a booth showing our signs and literature, in addition to distributing samples of prunes to the doctors. It was so different that it created a lot of attention and stories in the press. We were even featured on a few TV news segments. Even today, the American Heart Association literature includes prune literature. The Board members were quite pleased with all the extra, positive attention to how healthy prunes were.

Chapter 12

THE GOLDEN PRUNE AWARD

Ronnie Schell was a tremendously talented comedian and actor. One day, I was watching the Dinah Shore talk show and there was Ronnie talking about making breakfast in a blender. I learned from that show that Ronnie was a health enthusiast.

He said that there were certain foods that you have to put into the blender, including mango, strawberry, prunes and peanut butter. That was his "must" list of ingredients. This was terrific for us... someone talking about healthy prunes on national television. He served it to Dinah and her guests and they all said it tasted great.

We decided to contact him to see if we could create some publicity for him... and our prune client. We met at our office and thanked him for promoting prunes We said we'd like to give him an award that we will call the "Golden Prune Award." We had never done that before. We just made it up on the spot.

We had a company that makes our plaques paint a prune with gold paint and create a plaque, which said, " To Ronnie Schell, the Golden Prune Award for drawing attention to good nutrition through humor." We took publicity photos and sent it out to the media.

We knew that from then on, Ronnie was going to promote his healthy blender breakfast drink and talked about prunes, saying that, "prunes are good for you." It occurred to us, why stop here? Let's go further while we have this opportunity.

We called Dinah's producer and told him that we'd like to present this award to Ronnie on Dinah's show. Miss Golden Prune, Karen Lindsey, could also appear on the show to make the presentation. The producer loved the idea. Karen was attractively dressed in a fashionable gown. Dinah introduced her on the show and said, "Ronnie, Miss Prune would like to give you an award." Karen presented him with the award and read the inscription out loud. Then, he and Dinah started talking to Karen all about prunes.

That's when the fun really started. Ronnie said to Karen, "How long have you been Miss Prune?" She said, "Three years." He said, "Is that a 'running title?'" Then he said, "How did you become Miss Prune?" She said, "It was a process of elimination." Well, that tore the house down because he said, "Well, you got me there." Then she said, "Ronnie, in your honor, we've given a box of California prunes to everybody in the audience." He quickly added, "I wish you hadn't done that until we were off the air…." One joke followed another and it was quite a humorous segment with several double en tendres about prunes.

Ronnie, who was very interested in good nutrition got serious and asked Miss Prune to talk about how healthy prunes are. She said they were rich in vitamin A, low in sodium and high in potassium. Dinah added that she had prune recipes in her cookbook, including a prune whip and prunes in port wine. Ronnie added, "Would you like a prune whip?" To which Karen replied, "I'll keep the prunes and you keep the whip." Dinah laughed so hard that she couldn't catch her breath, while the audience was screaming with laughter.

It was like a 15-minute commercial, with the three of them having fun and talking about prunes and nutrition. You couldn't pay for that much publicity. It was incredible.

We knew that our prune industry client would enjoy the publicity, even though they may have been sensitive about some of the prune jokes. But, we figured how could you get on a national TV show and get so much publicity without stirring up a little controversy?

So, that was an adventure in PR that turned out pretty well and another example of taking advantage of an opportunity that landed right in front of us.

Chapter 13

BIN LADEN KILLS SALMON PROMOTION

The California Salmon Council operates under the State Department of Food and Agriculture and it represents all the California commercial salmon fishermen. Once a year, when the new season starts, the fishermen are able to go out and catch fish in specific areas. The government informs them when they can fish and how much they can catch. They're very careful about what they call "sustainability," making sure there is enough salmon left at the end of the season to help start the next season. Salmon season is something that the foodies, the restaurant owners and retailers, as well as many people who just love salmon, look forward to. It's a short season. It starts May 1 and runs through the end of August.

Every year, as the PR agency, it is our job to get the word out and create some publicity and enthusiasm so people know about it, and also let the retailers know that we're promoting salmon, so they can feature it and put it in their specials. What we usually do, working with the manager of the Salmon Council and working with the promotion committee, is plan ahead to see what we can tell people about the salmon taste, how delicious it is, how healthy it is and how it's now available.

We usually start at the end of March and work during the month of April, preparing releases, background stories, recipes, website information and literature. We contact the media in advance to inform them when the season starts and would they like to give us an interview with a commercial fisherman right from the boat? Maybe they'd like to talk with the chairman of the Salmon Council or our chef, home economist or our dietitian for various health and nutrition ideas. It's a full month of making arrangements and then at the last minute we wait for the official word from the government telling us to begin our activities.

This seemed a normal year and we had all the information out. In fact, this year was supposed to be a relatively good year. May 1 arrived. That's the day that the media already had our releases and information. But guess what? In 2011, May 1 was the day that Osama Bin Laden was assassinated! Can you imagine that? No news happened in the newspapers or on radio or TV or on the Internet, except coverage of the assassination. We were wiped off the map, along with every other news story. Our news was certainly not as important as Bin Laden being assassinated. What a disaster for us.

The media had the background video we produced, as well as our news releases. It was total chaos for us, as you know, something like that certainly is not a one day story. This story went on for at least three or four weeks solid.

We now had to find some way of getting back into the news. We realized we lost the excitement of the opening day, but we still wanted to talk about what's going on with salmon. So, we rewrote and updated our stories and changed our approach so that we could go back to the media, back to the retailers, back to the restaurant owners and actually be honest with them and say we got off to a slow start. But now, everything is going full speed with salmon season.

That gave us something to talk about, so we actually contacted the press all over again and wrote a new release and sent new letters, and said "California fishermen got off to a slow start. But now, they're going full speed," and repeated all the good things we previously said about the salmon.

Well, it worked out okay, even with a slow start. We didn't get the volume of stories we expected. But, at least we survived. We were able to continue on until the end of the season fizzled out.

The point to remember is, the Bin Laden was a huge and unexpected occurrence. We had no control over it whatsoever. We were in trouble for a few weeks. But we had to recuperate. You just can't quit and tell your clients you're sorry. All you can do is mark it off as an adventure that is not too pleasant, but show that you can survive.

Chapter 14

WHERE IS THE SHRIMP?

ere's an adventure that occurred because of a mishap. A delivery man's mistake almost caused a marketing disaster for our client.

We were promoting Ocean Garden Mexican Shrimp and, at this particular time, we were participating in the most important food service industry trade show, the American Culinary Federation. This took place in Atlantic City. Chefs, restaurant operators and food service buyers attend to learn about the products available and make buying decisions. Our client planned way in advance of the show to have a large exhibit with freezers to display the various shrimp products with stoves to cook and demonstrate the various recipes and presentations by a recognized chef all to create greater sales. For this particular show, we created the Ocean Garden Shrimp Cook-Off and the event would be part of the show's scheduled events. The winning chefs would receive $5,000 in cash, trips to Mexico and many other valuable prizes, in addition to being recognized for their cooking skills.

Prior to the convention, many chefs presented their recipes that were judged by well-known master chefs. They chose 8 finalists who would prepare their recipes in front of the audience and would be judged by well-recognized chefs.

Here's where the adventure began. Our client's staff and I flew from California the Friday before the opening day to prepare for the show. Usually, frozen products are stored in large refrigerated trucks and the exhibitors obtain their product to put in the freezers in their booth. I would do all of the pre arrangements for the press to visit the exhibit and make the necessary arrangements for the contest that would take place the opening day. When we went to pick up the shrimp, there were none to be found. "Where is the shrimp?" became the slogan of the day.

With the help of show management, we searched the premises and the other exhibits to see if perhaps someone had taken our product by mistake. We found that was not the case. After many phone calls to home base and the trucking company, we discovered that the truck driver delivered the shrimp to the wrong address. To make things worse, it was to a different city located many miles from Atlantic City.

Again, after many phone calls to see how we could get the shrimp, we were able to make arrangements for it to arrive hopefully by Saturday, early afternoon. In the meantime, we made arrangements with the show's management to change the schedule to late in the day so that the chefs would be able to have sufficient time to get the shrimp ready for their contest. We only had a few hours. This meant communicating with all of the visitors, with information about the change in schedule. We had a few hours after the opening without our shrimp in the exhibit. In addition, I had to track down the writers and reporters, with whom I had set up specific interviews with our client at the exhibit.

This really was 24-hours of frustration, anxiety and embarrassment. Although, it was interesting to note, Where's the Ocean Garden Shrimp? was the talk of the show. The shrimp was delivered, the contest was a huge success and Ocean Garden certainly had extra exposure and visitors knew exactly where to go to taste the high quality shrimp. It worked out well, despite the mishap.

Chapter 15

GRANDE CALAMARI, SQUID BY ANY OTHER NAME

One year, Mother Nature surprised the Mexican fishing industry and provided a tremendous oversupply of giant squid. The industry's marketing department had to make an immediate decision. The fisherman were bringing squid in by the tons and they had never marketed squid before. Suddenly it became a new product, which meant a "new product introduction." They had to take advantage of the tremendous supply that they had and immediately start working on deciding how they were going to market it.

Now they had to move quickly because it was a matter of finances. They had to pay for storage and had to do all the fishing of the product when it's available. So it was tremendously important for them to work quickly.

Well, they did. They were very bright people and they came up with several plans. Number one, squid is not too exciting as far as marketing. So they called it "Calamari," which is the Italian word for squid. It's recognized officially by the government that squid could be called Calamari. Because the calamari were large, with large tenticles, they decided to call it "Grande Calamari."

They were fishing and bringing it in with a rush job to introduce the product. The first thing they decided to do was have us, as their marketing and home economist department, get recipes, take food photos and provide them with advertising in the seafood journals, in literature and direct mail to the chefs, basically everything to let everyone know about the Grande Calamari.

Our first task was to find very famous, top chefs, to develop recipes for us. The chefs were pleased because they got personal publicity and being artists, they like to show off their own talents.

We were fortunate in Los Angeles, as there were several very prominent chefs, nationally known, that we contacted. I chose four chefs. One was Bernard Jacoby, a famous chef from France, who was the Executive Chef of the Biltmore Hotel in downtown Los Angeles. He was thrilled to do it and told me to come back at the end of the week. I came back and he had left for Paris, but left a large envelope for me.

I was very pleased and ran back to the office and opened up the envelop to give it to my home economist to start preparing for the photo, and guess what? The recipe was written in French. It never occurred to me to say "write it in English." Of course, it caused a problem. We had to find a French chef immediately who could interpret the ingredients and had to find a very technical translation service to see that everything was perfectly translated and presented so people could read it in English. It worked, even though it took a lot of time. But that was just our first blow.

We quickly took some food photos for seafood and restaurant trade journals. In order to present a new product, you had to have a big kick-off event. We decided to have a food industry luncheon in San Francisco and also another luncheon in Las Vegas.

While everything ran smoothly in San Francisco, our second blow came in Las Vegas. Las Vegas is known as a fashion setting for food all over the country because it has many tremendous hotels with very fine restaurants and chefs. That is a fast way of showing off recipes and acceptance. The Mexican seafood industry's marketing department made arrangements at Bally's Hotel in Las Vegas for a giant luncheon. There is an organization in Las Vegas called Chefs De Cuisine, a very prestigious chefs organization and they had all the members invited, and of course, we invited the media, as well.

We had literature, we had photos, we had presentations, we had video, everything you could think of to let them get enthusiastic and excited about accepting the new product, Grande Calamari.

We flew out from Los Angeles the night before. The first thing we did was go into the kitchen with our client's marketing director. We spoke to the Bally's chef and he said he received our product and it's being thawed out in the refrigerator. He said, "Tomorrow, in the early morning, I will start preparing the recipes as you instructed us to, and we're all set to go." Luckily, we got there early in the morning and the chef said, "We're going to start working on it right now." My marketing manager walked over to the box in the refrigerator and she almost fainted. I asked what was wrong and she said "They sent us the wrong squid." How could we have gotten the wrong squid? Squid is squid. She said "No, it has to be tenderized. The shipping department sent the first phase of the squid. We have our own tenderizing machines."

I learned then, that squid happened to be one of the food products that has to be tenderized. I noticed in various events that chefs tenderize veal and things like that, by pounding it with mallets with steel buttons on the end of it. At the factory, they have electric driven points that pierce right into the calamari.

Well, the chef, who was very professional, didn't panic. He was certainly disappointed he had to do a lot of extra work, though. He immediately put his staff together and they all started pounding the calamari. It was really funny to watch. But they were doing it and I guess that's a normal procedure with certain foods. But, of course, it would have not taken much time if it was pre-pounded. It made them a little bit late for lunch. But the food was terrific. Everybody was pleased and everything worked out great. There were many compliments about the new Grande Calamari product.

Now again, we stopped to analyze who was wrong, what happened and how did it happen. The shipping department was careless and they had taken the original Calamari that came before it had been pounded, and they had not sent the right boxes. So again, you can't assume anything and at least, you've got to double check everything when you're dealing with someone else providing another part of the program that you are working on. Had they taken one minute longer, the shipping department would've shipped the correct pounded product. But, it worked out fine, thank goodness and it was a great promotion plus, a tremendous marketing success.

Chapter 16

DISASTER AVOIDED AT MEXICAN PRESIDENT'S VISIT

Years ago, the President of Mexico, Luis Echeverria, was planning to a trip to California, which would be highlighted with a visit, from then, Governor Reagan. They would highlight the good neighbor policies and commerce between their two countries. It was an important visit, especially for California business.

Governor Reagan's staff started preparing for a huge dinner and a reception to be held at the famous Century Plaza Hotel, in Los Angeles, that would be attended by many civic officials, dignitaries, business executives and of course, the press. This event was of most interest to our client, Ocean Garden Products, distributors of shrimp from Mexico. This company was owned and operated by the Mexican Government Fisheries Department, which was located in San Diego. Since the company was owned by the Mexican government, it was most important for them to be involved, especially for the San Diego executives, to impress the visiting Mexican officials and demonstrate their presence in America.

The president of Ocean Garden asked us to do everything possible to see that they were represented and highly visible at this dinner. He wanted to make sure that he and his company executives could attend the dinner and be seated close to the head table, so the Mexican President could see them participating in this event. Since they would be talking about commerce, we would do everything possible to see that Ocean Garden Mexican Shrimp was in the "news." We contacted the Governor's office and were able to make arrangements for the group from San Diego to be highly visible at the event.

In dealing with our general contacts, we decided the food served would no doubt be talked about in the stories coming out of this event. We contacted the catering department at the Century Plaza Hotel and advised them that we represented the Mexican Government Fisheries Division and would like to see the planned menu. Of course, just like any major event, when people are talking about what will be served it becomes a news item and an opportunity to show that Mexican shrimp was a major ingredient, highlighted on the menu.

Much to our surprise and the shock to the staff at the Century Plaza, we discovered that the beautiful menus they printed, describing the events, had listed the first item as Louisiana shrimp cocktail. Somebody really goofed! Can you imagine the embarrassment, the shock and the negative impression that would have made while trying to honor the trade activities between Mexico and California if a competitive shrimp was highlighted? It would have been a diplomatic disaster. Luckily for us, the hotel staff was able to move quickly and reprint the menus in time. And, of course, ensure they had a sufficient amount of the Mexican shrimp available. You can say, we actually saved the day.

The Governor's staff was so pleased that we discovered the error, they gave us much more privileges at the event. Our client was invited to the private reception, prior to the dinner, where he could personally meet with Governor Reagan and President Echeverria, and impress the Mexican President with the fact that Ocean Garden Products were recognized as part of the commerce in the United States. We benefited, too. My son, Howard, and I attended and were able to meet with this select group of government officials and dignitaries. At the dinner, the Mexican President, was pleased to see the large Ocean Garden staff greeting him as he entered the stage.

The menu items of the dinner were picked up in the news. Ocean Garden Products and the Mexican Government Fisheries Department both became part of the story in both the regular press and the food industry trade magazines. Personal interaction between the Mexican President and our client, and the high visibility at the dinner, was a huge success. It definitely showed how when faced with something negative, you can turn it into something positive. Our client was extremely pleased with our activities.

Chapter 17

SMOKED WHITEFISH, A GIANT RECALL

One day, the headline news came out with a tragedy. Three people in Tennessee died from botulism, eating smoked fish. The government investigators discovered that that particular product came from Lake Eerie and possibly the processor did not smoke it to the desired temperature that would kill the bacteria. The fish that came from that area was immediately recalled from markets.

Our client, the Los Angeles Smoking and Curing Company, was the largest distributor of smoked seafood in the West. Even though their product did not come from Lake Eerie, they suffered the consequences. The consumers and retailers, reacting to the story, stopped buying the white fish and other smoked items. Even though our client's product came from other areas and was properly processed to the correct temperature, it took almost a year for sales to resume. And, our client and other processors, had serious financial losses.

Here is where the adventure begins. As I'm sure you've noticed, the press, many times, brings up anniversaries of past events. The Saturday Evening Post, one of the most popular magazines, came out with a story describing the one year anniversary of that sad event. Once again, the bad news affected our client's sales. As his public relations agency, he asked us to do something about it right away. That's a difficult chore. He actually wanted us to "insist" that the Saturday Evening Post write a retraction. We knew from past experience that, in most cases, they wouldn't and if they did, that would only bring more attention to the original story. However, perhaps we could do something new with the Saturday Evening Post, in a positive way. At least we could show our client that we were trying.

It just so happened that I was going to New York to promote several of our California commodities. I visited the magazine's editor and told him about the consequences of their story and asked if there was any way that we could provide material that would have reader acceptance and help our product sales. I suggested recipes, food photos and stories pertaining to, not only smoked fish, but several of our California products, such as, turkeys, wine, fruits and vegetables. Sometimes, one gets lucky and is at the right place at the right time. This is one instance.

The editor told me that they were actually preparing a barbeque story and were almost at the end. Their theme was what some of the celebrities and well-known people do for their barbeques. That was a great break for us and I suggested that we come up with some material for them from California. They said they would consider it, but we had to move quickly. We immediately went into action.

Since we represented the California turkey industry, we came up with the idea of having a barbequed turkey with all the trimmings. After many phone calls and meetings, we were able to get California Governor, Pat Brown, and his wife, to let us plan a barbeque for them. If the feature was accepted it would certainly give California, the Governor and products, goodwill publicity. Working with Mrs. Brown, our home economist developed a complete menu, which included turkey with many fruits and vegetables, wine and smoked seafood. It was like making a movie. The idea was accepted by the Saturday Evening Post and they sent their top photographer out. Our staff prepared the entire menu and Governor Brown and his family graciously participated in the photo and story. Our clients were delighted. It was a very popular issue and a most successful and pleasant adventure. Once again, we proved that you can approach problems with honey rather than vinegar. Our client was very pleased with the positive publicity we received for his fish products.

Chapter 18

ZSA ZSA SAYS NO

One day in the mid-80s, our friend and associate in New York called up and gave us an assignment. She had just been retained by Pick, the largest Hungarian salami company in Hungary. Her job was to reintroduce this product to the U.S.A. It was previously banned for import to the U.S.A through WWII, due to the chaos and problems of the Cold War with Russia. This went on for over 50 years. It was called the "red curtain." Finally, the "red curtain" was lifted and many of the countries were now able to export their products to the U.S.A. Thus, it was really called a "reintroduction." At this particular time, the famous Fancy Food Show, a trade show geared towards the market retailers, which was taking place in Los Angeles, and was a perfect venue to reach the retailers and advise them that Hungarian Salami is "back."

We were to aid Pick's sales department and garner as much publicity as possible, mostly, to the retail trade and then to the consumers. We were to do the traditional contact with the press and find ways of generating stories about the product and encourage attendees of the Fancy Food Show to visit the Pick exhibit and learn about the availability and prices and, of course, taste the delicious Salami. My son,

Howard, who handled the account with me, came up with a terrific idea that would make an impression on both the retailers and the consumers. Here's where the adventure begins.

Zsa Zsa Gabor, the famous Hungarian actress, was as popular then as Kim Kardashian is now. She was famous for just "being" famous. The press would follow her wherever she went. Everyone was interested in her daily life. She was famous for her Hungarian accent, for her clothes, her expensive jewelry, her lovers and her crazy antics. There was no internet then, but if there was, I'm sure she would have many millions of followers.

Howard decided that we should have a Zsa Zsa Gabor "look alike contest" and publicize it to the trade media and consumers. We chose a theater across the street from the convention hall to put on the event. We would hire one of Hollywood's top caterers to serve the Hungarian salami, as creatively as possible. It made good sense from a publicity point of view.

So, we first contacted Zsa Zsa and told her what we were doing and invited her to be a judge. Much to our surprise, she said she was not interested at all. She didn't want to be associated with salami, but considering all the crazy things she did, it didn't make sense to us. Not only that, she actually threatened to sue us if we used her name and she would sue everyone connected with the salami. That caused a problem and because of our eagerness to develop this project we had already contacted the press to tell them about what we were planning to do and we had already started making arrangements for a Zsa Zsa look alike contest.

After brainstorming and discussing the pros and cons we decided that since Zsa Zsa was basically in public domain, she couldn't really sue us. But to respect her wishes, we still went along with the contest and now called it "The Famous Hungarian Movie Star Look Alike Contest." Everyone would still know it was Zsa Zsa. We went ahead with it. Since we were in Hollywood, we had no trouble getting contestants. There were dozens of young actresses that entered the contest for publicity and attention. Some of them were terrific. They dressed, talked and acted like Zsa Zsa.

We had several radio and TV personalities as judges and we included Ron Smith, whose agency provided actor look a-likes for special events. One of the prizes was going to be a listing with his agency that would get them jobs at the special events that used lots of look a-likes. For the first prize we were able to get a deluxe trip to Hungary with all the extras. The Hungarian government Travel Bureau gave us the award because they realized it would get a tremendous amount of publicity. The exhibitors were all talking about it and we planned the event in the early evening, after the exhibits at the trade show were closed, so that many more people could attend. The press wrote about it and talked about it in advance. They also attended the event, which was a huge success. It was covered by radio, television and newspapers. The winner and two runner-ups, subsequently, had many jobs appearing as Zsa Zsa.

Johnny Gilbert seeing triple – Zsa Zsas, that is, (l. to r.) winner, Pat La Pearl, runnerup Helga and second runnerup, Temah Martel.

The publicity did not stop there. It went on and on. The next day everyone was talking about it at the trade show. The attendees made extra visits to the Pick exhibit to sample the salami and talk about the event. When the winner left for her trip, there was press interest when she left, when she arrived in Hungary and when she returned.

We did not hear from Zsa Zsa, but I'm sure she was pleased to hear her name over and over again. It was fun and very productive. It turned out to be an asset and gave us twice as much publicity. Could you have imagined what would have happened if we had internet? It certainly would have gone viral. It was an extremely successful adventure and our New York associate and, of course, the client, were very pleased with our results.

Chapter 19

BOB HOPE, A TRUE CLASSIC

We represented the California Grapefruit Growers Association, whose orchards were located in Coachella Valley, a few miles south of Palm Springs. Our job was to get consumers to be aware of and to buy California grapefruit, as opposed to grapefruit from Florida or Texas. During the season, we would do the usual public relations activities to encourage consumers to purchase more grapefruit and, of course, ensure it was from California. In looking for various themes, it occurred to us that Palm Springs was in the news often, due to celebrities flocking there and was very recognizable, certainly more so than Coachella Valley. We were seeking sources that would help us connect Palm Springs with the grapefruit.

This adventure turned out to be a perfect tie-in with the Bob Hope Desert Golf Classic. We did something for Bob Hope and he did something for us. It was such a successful promotion that it repeated for the next 8 years.

This annual golfing fundraiser utilized four different nearby golf courses. Bob's favorite charity was the Eisenhower Medical Center, in Palm Springs. He donated all of the land on which the Center was built. He constantly sought means of helping them raise money. Once a year, he sponsored this popular golf classic, which was very well-known in the sport's press and had many of the celebrities, sports figures, civic officials and other popular people participate. It was televised with thousands of visitors in attendance. It raised a lot of money for his charity.

Since this event took place during our growing season, with Bob Hope being so popular, we thought it would be a perfect tie-in. So we came up with several ideas and presented it to Bob's publicity agent. We suggested that we could publicize the golf tournament with our media connections, which were different outlets than their usual sports and news media. We now had photos and recipes from Bob Hope pertaining to grapefruit. We would get additional publicity in areas that usually didn't get covered, like general press publicity and especially with food editors. We suggested that we could have a favorite grapefruit recipe from Bob and have a photo session with him and release it all over to draw attention to the fact that the recipe would be featured in connection with the golf tournament. Since it would help publicize the event, Bob was pleased to do it. And that started a whole series of publicity events that drew attention to Coachella Valley California grapefruit, as well as the Golf Classic.

The classy Mr. Hope, checking out the grapefruits.

It just so happened that Bob did have a favorite grapefruit recipe. It was very simple. It was broiled grapefruit, cut in half, with honey and cornflakes sprinkled on top. And then cooked briefly in the broiler. It was very tasty. We took photos of Bob with the grapefruit.

We also had three very attractive model/actresses wearing yellow T-shirts saying "I'm a Coachella Valley Grapefruit Lover," who posed for publicity photos with many of the celebrities at the event. We supplied grapefruit to the chefs at the hotels where the contestants and guests were staying. We supplied stories and recipes to many newspapers. We also mentioned it in our many food-related interviews on radio and TV.

We officially attended this huge event and received official press badges so we could get up close and personal with all of the participants in the tournament with our grapefruit girls posing for photos. We positioned our grapefruit girls at the ninth hole, so we could meet and greet the celebrities as they played through and took as many photos as we could. Photographers representing the press from around the world were in attendance and our grapefruit girls got in a tremendous amount of publicity photos getting a great amount of exposure for our grapefruit client. The grapefruit girls even posed for photos with Bob Hope and President Gerald Ford among the many celebrities.

Andy Williams relaxed and ready to swing.

One of the many chefs serving grapefruit to tournament participants has a photo op.

President Ford and the "Grapefruit Girls" with Howard Pearlstein (r.) setting up the photo shoot.

Johnny Bench, baseball great.

Comic Flip Wilson

Jack Nicklaus, the "Golden Bear" and the "Golden Girls" of Grapefruit.

During the week of the event Bob had several major interviews about what was going on with the golf tournament and he mentioned that he met and posed with the Coachella Valley grapefruit girls and, in some cases even mentioned his favorite grapefruit recipe. Some of the major retailers in Los Angeles and in the surrounding areas put up huge displays of Coachella Valley grapefruit and connected it with the Bob Hope Dessert Golf Classic. California grapefruit was in the news before, during and after the event. This helped raise money for the Eisenhower Medical Center. Bob Hope and our client were both very pleased with this fun and exciting tie-in adventure. We couldn't have asked for anything more!

Chapter 20

O.J. SIMPSON FOILS OUR PROMOTION

ere's an event that happened which we had no control over that ruined a complete promotion. We were just putting the finishing touches on a publicity program that we developed for the Fourth of July. Holidays were always a good source for us with heavy interest in foods. We would find ways of communicating with the press with ideas on food preparation and handy tips for this specific holiday. We would include several of our food products that were compatible and that would fit in with our theme for the holidays. This time we were concentrating on picnics, outdoor barbeque's and fun entertainment. We prepared many recipes and suggestions and handy hints, helping the consumer prepare their foods in an easy manner, and of course, present their guests with fine tasting food. In addition to the usual food editor releases, because of the interest in the Fourth of July, we were able to schedule several radio and television interviews.

Our theme this year was how to have a barbequed turkey dinner, showing how to prepare the turkey and all of the add-ons. In that case, we could promote our client, Mrs. Cubbison's stuffing mix, as an important side dish. And, as an alternative, so that we could promote our California Wild- Caught Salmon, we also had many ways of preparation and easy-to-cook recipes. We obtained props to fit the occasion and we prepared the many food dishes that would be shown on TV.

As we were preparing for the first show in the middle of June, there was breaking news that saturated the media for days and days. In fact, later on, months and months. It was the murder case that involved O.J. Simpson, the famous football player accused of killing his ex-wife, Nicole Brown and Ronald Goldman, a so-called friend. As you can imagine, our soft news was completely eliminated. We had communicated with the grocery trade about the entire promotion. They had already created massive displays of our products and there was nothing we could do about it, now. The media was so totally dedicated to this shocking event that they even pre-empted their popular specialty shows, such as the Food News show. The sad thing for us was that we could not repeat the theme since it was directly related to the Fourth of July. Then, when O.J. Simpson was arrested and the trial started, everyday for many months, the news was totally dedicated to the trial.

How could we recupe and bounce back? We hoped that the trial news would slow down and we could take advantage of the next food holiday, which was Labor Day. So, we regrouped and revamped our program and converted the radio and TV activities, for the Fourth of July suggestions into Labor Day suggestions. We did lose the advantage of the very heavy shopping days for the Fourth of July, but at least we were able to get the benefit of the Labor Day activities.

It certainly proves that a murder can cause the death of a normal story.

Chapter 21

SNOOPY FOR PRESIDENT

Snoopy, without a doubt, was one of the most loved characters in the country. Not only the country, but in the world. Snoopy was happy, friendly and funny. That's why our client, Interstate Bakeries Company (Weber's Bread and Dolly Madison Cakes) decided to make Snoopy their mascot and used this character in all of their promotions. It was a perfect character to go with their white bread, popularly used for sandwiches, especially for kids' lunches. They went ahead and put Snoopy on their bread and cake wrappers. They had signs, photos and fun things, all about Snoopy. They had a Snoopy costume and part of our promotion was to have the Snoopy character appear at special events, at which time, we distributed the photos and other materials. It was a fun promotion. Snoopy was very popular.

We had a modest advertising budget and mostly used radio. One day, we were visiting KLAC radio, which was one of the leading stations in Los Angeles, and we learned they were getting ready for a really big event. It was the Ontario 500 race, which was going to take place at the Ontario Speedway just outside of Los Angeles and recognized as one of the biggest car racing events of the year. They were making arrangements to promote the event and fill the stadium and were also going to broadcast "live" at the event. We discovered they were going to have a pre-auto parade and have a Grand Marshall, music and dignitaries to add to the excitement and entertainment. They told us they had arranged for Buzz Aldrin, the famous astronaut, to be the Grand Marshall.

We asked if we could get involved with Snoopy somehow and reminded them that as a promotional gimmick, Snoopy was running for President that year, competing with Ronald Regan and Jimmy Carter, it was a fun promotion that we created. Could they make Snoopy a dignitary at the event? They immediately said yes and saw the opportunities for entertainment, so we decided to go further and asked if, perhaps Snoopy could be a co-Grand Marshall with Buzz Aldrin and be in the beginning of the auto parade? They said it would be OK with them, but they would have to check with the producers of the show and Buzz Aldrin. A day later they came back to us and said Buzz was very pleased and he considered that a great addition. What a terrific opportunity. That was the beginning of a very exciting adventure.

We immediately started making plans to put the project together. We found a college girl at a temp agency who lived near the speedway and told her we had a Snoopy costume and would have her change at her home and pick her up and drive her to the event and drive her back afterwards. Then, we had to find a convertible that Snoopy could be in and wave at everyone. We created a sign that said "Snoopy for President," sponsored by Weber's Bread, for the side of the car. Much to our surprise it was hard to find a convertible from a car dealer and had to go to a car rental. We found one that had a vintage 1979 cadillac, which looked great. We found out that anything that could have gone wrong with the car did. It was a total lemon.

My sons, Frank and Howard, picked the car up and started out at 7:30AM that Sunday morning. It was very cold and they decided to put the top up for comfort. The first thing that happened was the handle to the back door fell off. That was a bad omen. When they started the car, they were not able to connect the top properly and struggled to make it fit. When they finally connected it, they were worried they would not be able to open the top again. On the freeway, as they were speeding along, suddenly, large plumes of heavy black smoke poured out of the tail pipe. They were sure they would get in trouble with the Highway Patrol and annoy the other drivers on the freeway. Then, the car started to rattle and they thought perhaps they were driving too fast, so they cut down the speed. Finally, they got down to as low as 25 miles an hour. The car stopped rattling and the smoke was not as thick. They discovered at even 25 miles an hour, all sorts of sounds were happening. It just didn't seem right.

Time was going by and they knew they had to pick up the model in the Snoopy costume soon and be at the stadium in time for the auto parade, prior to the big race. They kept pushing ahead. The car sputtered again and they figured they should get off the freeway and check it out. As they were exiting the freeway the car completely stalled out. Fortunately, there was a gas station at the bottom of the exit and they had to put the car in neutral and push it the rest of the way down the ramp. They didn't expect to find a mechanic Sunday morning, but luckily the attendant helped them get the car started again. They opened the hood, steam rushed out and they, of course, discovered that the radiator was empty. While they were letting the car rest they found a public phone to call the model who was probably worried to death about them not being there, yet.

They told her they were running late and would head out as soon as the car was cooled off and ready to go. There were no cell phones in those days, so it was very inconvenient. After they were able to start the car again, they managed to get to the model's house. They rushed to the Speedway and they barely arrived on time. They were immediately ushered in and put at the front of the parade with Buzz. The music started, the parade started and the television cameras were rolling and the radio station was broadcasting "live."

Snoopy greets 30,000 race fans, while Howard drives and prays
the old Caddie doesn't die during the pre-race parade.

In order to avoid any complications, Howard drove the vintage Cadillac slower than usual, praying that the car would not stall out in front of the entire parade. They slowly progressed around the track with the fans waving and cheering and there was a lot of photo-taking. Everything turned out fine, as the car made it around the track and didn't die out in front of everybody. The participation of Snoopy, on behalf of our client, was a huge success. The two PR brothers were totally exhausted and happy that the huge event, with the jinxed car, was finally over. The end result of this wild adventure was that we received a tremendous amount of positive publicity for our client and their products.

Chapter 22

WILD HONEY, A WILD PROMOTION

We were promoting Superior Honey for the leading independent honey company in Southern California. We were getting
ready for National Honey Week. That's an excuse to get extra
publicity. As we were getting ready, in the Los Angeles Harold
Express, there was a photo of a very attractive young lady holding
a record album with the words, "Wild Honey." That surprised us
and we questioned, was somebody else competing with us? We
didn't know about "Wild Honey" and thought perhaps it was in-
terfering with our publicity. We called the editor and asked about
that particular photo. He told us that it was released by Capitol
Records.

John Arsesi poses with "Miss Wild Honey" (Marguerite
Barbera) and his recording of "Wild Honey."

We called Capitol Records and we asked them what this was all
about. They told us they had a new singer, John Arcesi and he just
did a record album, which was called "Wild Honey." The publicity
department was promoting the album. We suggested that perhaps we
could work together. After all, we were promoting National Honey
Week, which was coming up and they could promote the album at
the same time. After a long brainstorming session, we came up with
a combined promotional program.

A simple approach was, we provided honey gift packs and some
general news about National Honey Week, along with their "Wild

Honey" albums to the radio DJs, who loved gimmicks like that. They gave us albums and we sent them to the buyers at the markets telling them that we were tieing in with Capitol Records who was helping us promote Superior Honey. That was fine. It certainly drew attention to our promotion. Then, the Capitol Records publicity man came up with a "wild" idea. He suggested that we have a honey and feather party at the famous Garden of Ala Hotel.

In honor of National Honey Week, we would create a beauty contest and would contact the DJs and the newspaper entertainment editors and invite them to the party. They would supply chicken feathers in little plastic bags (which we would obtain from one of our poultry accounts) and have the DJs blow the feathers on the contestants, beautiful models in bathing suits, coated with honey. That's the meaning of honey and feathers. They knew that honey is water-soluble and that the young ladies would be able to take a shower to get rid of the honey and feathers. That sounded crazy, but we went ahead with the idea and planned this party.

We made a large display of Superior Honey. We hired several models and gave them banners that had "Miss Superior Honey," "Miss Honey and Butter" and "Miss Clover Honey." In other words, names of our brands of honey and, of course, "Miss Wild Honey." The idea was that they would choose the Queen of Honey Week. Obviously, they would get exposure for Miss Wild Honey, promoting John Arcesi and his record album, while we would benefit from it with our publicity exposure. In addition, we would be able to follow up with the grocery trade publications with stories and photos relating to the Superior Honey promotion and encourage the retailers to make displays and feature Superior Honey.

Honey and Record Promotion

Spencer Redfield, sales manager of Superior Honey Co., surrounded by a group of Superior Honeys at the recent Honey-and-Feather party in honor of National Honey Week.

Superior Honey Co. recently tied in with Capitol Records and John Arcesi during National Honey Week to promote honey and the Capitol record, "Wild Honey."

Leo Pearlstein, president of Lee & Associates, handled all the details for this very successful promotion.

It all started with a picture of "Miss Wild Honey" in the newspapers. Upon investigation, Mr. Pearlstein discovered that Capitol Records was embarking upon a publicity campaign to promote Johnnie Arcesi, one of their new singers, and his record, "Wild Honey."

The publicity men of the respective organizations decided to use the impetus of National Honey Week to jointly promote Superior Honey and Capitol Records.

One hundred leading disc jockeys, editors, etc., received personal invitations to a honey-and-feather party, at which event John Arcesi was to crown Miss Superior Honey, to be chosen from a bevy of Hollywood's most beautiful honeys: Miss Jellied Honey, Miss Honey Butter, Miss Sage Honey, Miss Clover Honey, Miss Creamed Honey, Miss Comb Honey, etc.

The newsreels and columnists turned out en masse, releasing a multitude of news releases pertaining to this event and National Honey Week.

The TV newsreels and news rooms broadcast this news as well.

The grocery trade was informed of the promotion so that they could tie in and take full advantage.

Grocery trade feature letting the industry
know about the honey promotion.

Our clients were very conservative and were worried about the honey and feather part. But after much discussion, they authorized it. They gave us money to pay the models. Being marketers, they actually became enthusiastic and invited several of their key buyers showing the grocery industry how active Superior Honey was in promoting their product. We had several very attractive young ladies that paraded around the pool and the DJs poured the honey on them. One of the DJs may have had a little bit too much to drink and poured honey on Miss Wild Honey's head. Yuck! That certainly drew a lot of attention. It looked pretty sticky to us.

Honey and feathers – a rare combination.

She was very upset so she ran up to her room to shower and she was able to get the honey out of her hair. You can imagine how the press reacted. They kept clicking their cameras and the video kept rolling.

I must tell you before we go further, I was a little worried, even though I like stunts. We decided to take a one time event insurance policy. We were worried that someone might trip on our honey display or fall into the pool. Unexpected things happen, but we did have insurance that came in handy later.

While Miss Wild Honey was showering, the Associated Press reporter was pushing us to do the judging because he had a deadline to meet and had to leave. He said he would write a big story if we would start now. Since Miss Wild Honey was showering, she was not in the line up. Miss Superior Honey, was chosen as the winner. Everything worked out very well for us. The Associated Press was happy and got a lot of photos. Generally, the party was a huge success.

A year later, Miss Wild Honey sued Superior Honey, Capital Records and the Garden of Ala Hotel, for her "experience" at the honey and feather contest. For some reason she didn't include us. She sued for $70,000 for the pouring of the honey on her head, for emotional disturbance and for losing the opportunity to be judged.

Model Seeks Damages for Honey and Feathers

First came the honey, then the feathers—Marguerite Barbera, 19, shuddered yesterday when she thought about it as she signed a $70,000 damage suit over her experience.

The complaint said that Miss Barbera, a tall and willowy model, was employed last Oct. 23 for a publicity stunt. She said she understood that her duties would consist only of donning a sketchy bathing suit and walking around the pool of a Hollywood hotel while a musical record of a crooner's voice was made.

Doused With Honey

But much to her chagrin and embarrassment, she said, suddenly a keg of honey was poured over her head and that was followed by a shower of feathers. She complained she was covered with the combination "from the crown of my head to the soles of my feet."

Her complaint, prepared by Atty. Bernard Lehrer, was directed against John Arcesi, the crooner; Pete Potter, disk jockey; Capitol Records, Inc; two press agents, Bud Freeman and Ed Scofield, and the Superior Honey Co. Miss Barbera sued through her mother, Mrs. Jeannette Barbera, 6028 Romain St.

At the time, Miss Barbera explained, she was playing the role of Miss Wild Honey and a recording of a song by the same name was in progress. The stunt was designed to publicize both the song and the product.

SUES — Miss Marguerite Barbera files honey and feather suit.

Times photo

A year later and our promotion was still in the news.

Our client was upset and we told them not to worry because we had an insurance policy in their name. Capitol Records who has a whole group of attorneys, who are use to being sued, said don't worry. She did this for publicity and never expected to get that much money. They sat down with the lawyers and ended up giving her only $70 each from the three companies that were sued. She got a tremendous amount of publicity. Photos were run of her again, the event was talked about, and here we were getting additional publicity a year later. All is well that ends well. Really… a "wild" adventure.

Chapter 23

CHINESE ACROBATIC TROOP

President Nixon visited China. That was world news. For the first time in decades it was the beginning of warming relations with the People's Republic of China. Everyone was watching the news to see what would happen. The first thing that happened after his visit was China sent over their ping pong players. The world soon found that, without a doubt, ping pong was their favorite sport and they were the world's best players. Then, they sent the Shen Yun Acrobatic Troop, which has never been seen outside of China. That was the viewing of a 5,000 year tradition. They performed at the Kennedy Center For The Performing Arts. It was an outstanding performance of music, costumes, beautiful dancers, Chinese history and acrobatics. It was unbelievable and was tremendously applauded by the audience.

Norton Simon, our client, grabbed the opportunity and they made arrangements to film the performance. They sponsored it on the national ABC television network. This was prestige, goodwill and just good advertising for the Norton Simon companies. They invested a tremendous amount of money in the production and wanted to carry through with as much publicity as possible to increase the viewing of the show.

They decided to have a giant preview dinner and show the film to publicize the TV show. They chose Los Angeles as their location. They asked us to handle all the PR and logistics. They would supervise from New York and have their executives attend the event.

They wanted to get the VIPs, the government officials, the music industry, entertainment industry and the retail food industry leaders to all come to the kickoff party before the television show. In other words, it was like having a world premiere. Our assignment was to do everything pertaining to this project. We were instructed to get the location for the party, make all arrangements for the party, including the menu and the preview showing of the acrobats. It was very exciting and good for our own prestige to supervise such a huge and important project.

We inherited one of client's staff from the agency who was not the easiest person to work with. He micro-managed us with constant phone calls and requests for every tiny detail. However, he was helpful, as he sent us a great deal of background information and instructions on arrangements that the client desired. We started immediately.

The first thing we did was to find a location for the party. We chose the Beverly Wilshire hotel, which was one of the most prestigious hotels in the city. It was large enough to handle a big crowd and fancy enough to service VIPs.

The next thing we had to do was to create an invitation list. The client sent us their choice and we added VIPs from the entertainment world, business and civic officials, in addition to a select media list. The client OK'd the list and we all agreed that this would probably be the party of the year. Everything seemed to be working out well and our supervisor, back in New York, kept calling every day and going through each event so he could keep in touch and see how things were progressing. We developed a checklist. He would go down the checklist and said, "OK, let's talk about the menu. How about the parking? How were the hotel arrangements? How about food serving suggestions?" He asked about all sorts of things that you do for a big party. And then he said, "What about the sound system?"

I have to tell you, that's one thing we knew from our many years of previous experience. We've been to events, great events, where everything was fine and the microphone didn't work or the sound system was bad. We were very proud of the fact that we had a soundman for double checking and were definitely sure that the sound will be perfect. We were rather proud of the fact that we could be ahead of them on that. He kept going down the list and got down to the projector. He said, "Ok, how is your projector? What's happening on that?" I answered, "Well, we've got one of the best projection people in the city. He's in charge. He's going to run it professionally and we are all set to go." So he said, "Well, what is your back up?" I said, "What back up? What do you mean?" He answered, "You have to have a back up. This is film. What happens if the film breaks? What happens if the light bulb goes out? We can't have an interruption on this very expensive project."

I said, that's why we have a professional doing it." He said, "No. I want a back up." Ok, so we called the projectionist up and told him. He said it was ok with him. He said, "Never did we have a problem like that. That's why I'm there." I asked, "So what do you do if something breaks?" He said, "I fix it immediately." I said, "Well, that's not good enough. The client wants another projector." He said, "OK, I'll have another projector. Get me another print of the film for it."

Evidently, what he did was have the two projectors facing the screen, focused together, and on the second projector, he ran the film at the same time without sound and without light.

Everything started and was working well. All of a sudden, believe it or not, right at a crucial point during the film, the first projector stopped. Never did he expect that. But, my client, back east, did! What the projectionist then did was press a button, which took less than a second and the second projector just kept going. Nobody in the audience even knew the film stopped at all. It just kept running and went through the entire show. Everyone applauded wildly. It was a beautiful presentation.

There you have it. The moral of this story is, be prepared and always have a back up. It was a very successful event. It worked out tremendously well. Everybody was happy. The TV show turned out to be one of the highest rated shows.

It could've been a huge disaster. Well, not really a disaster. But it could have been quite embarrassing. We were very lucky. We learned a lesson. Our client was right. If you're going to do something and it's important for production, double check everything. It was quite an adventure.

Chapter 24

ALCOA AND FOOD FOR THE ASTRONAUTS

We were very pleased to be retained by ALCOA (The Aluminum Company of America). We were to promote ALCOA aluminum foil in the Southern California area where they had very poor sales. They started late with their introduction and their competitors, Reynolds wrap and Kaiser, were both selling well. Even though Alcoa was heavily advertised, the retailers were reluctant to add another brand of foil. They asked us to do a very aggressive public relations program targeted both to the consumers and the retailers. They knew that we were very active in promoting turkeys and other food products and wanted to take advantage of our local contacts and our activities. We were very active and were making good progress.

One day, our client, the vice president of public relations, called and said he wanted us to do a special project. We were to go to New York and meet their promotion staff at the annual Food Editors Conference. This is a very important show attended by leading newspaper food editors in the country. Practically every major food company participates and sponsors various events, such as meals, presentations and demonstrations. They distribute samples of their products, food photos and recipes along with a great deal of printed material for the editors' use.

In order to stand out, ALCOA decided to sponsor a luncheon. They created a theme of the foods of tomorrow, all related to the first trip to the moon and the astronaut program. They created a menu of freeze-dried foods in aluminum containers that were similar to the astronauts' foods. They had a speaker from the government who explained the entire program. They prepared an aluminum-shaped missile to be placed at the entrance of the hall that the editors walk through and, the entire banquet room displayed photos and illustrations of the then "present and future" space program. The editors from the various states were seated together and various ALCOA executives were seated at each table. I was instructed to sit at the California table.

Here is where the adventure begins. The whole team, including the very top executives, arrived the evening before the convention was to start and went to the banquet hall to set up the missile and all of the artwork. Much to our surprise, and totally unexpected, there was a fundraiser dinner going on and we could not get in until the end, which was scheduled for midnight. What a setback! Obviously, we would have to come back after midnight and work until approximately 3:00AM to complete the project. The next morning a group of very tired public relations members prepared for the big luncheon. It was ready and the food editors came as scheduled.

The luncheon started and the speaker, a lady with a very dainty voice, started the presentation. She had only said a few words when suddenly, a horrific blast of music, with bongo drums and loud trumpets, came from the neighboring banquet room. What a shocker!

Everything came to a stop and several of the executives ran to the next room and discovered that this was the annual Caribbean Travel Association luncheon. Obviously, they were creating excitement and enthusiasm for their attendees. After pleading with them to stop the music, they agreed to adjust their program to help us. Even when things were calmed down, we still heard lots of noise from them. We lost our momentum. Naturally, it was most embarrassing. But we managed to complete the program.

I learned something then that helped me throughout my entire career. Never assume that everything is all set. Double check on everything connected with a planned event, especially outside interference. From then on, there were many times that we planned events and found that outside influence from the venue or the potential neighbors near where we were to be, could affect our program. So then, we did not choose those venues at that time and had our event elsewhere.

The end result of our ALCOA event was that we were able to draw a great deal of extra attention to the ALCOA brand name and its products.

Chapter 25

"ROCKY" MOVIE, HUGE SUCCESS

H ere's an adventure that started which had many twists and turns. It affected three clients. Before I get into it, let me tell you about the client that was involved in the beginning. We were very pleased to be appointed to handle the public relations and help introduce the famous Suntory Scotch Whiskey from Japan. Hardly anybody, either the consumers or the liquor industry, would expect to have scotch, especially to have a fine scotch, from Japan. The Japanese had a great deal of patience and did not expect to have tremendous results. They just wanted to go slowly and get distribution in the bars and liquor stores for their famous, premium Suntory Royal whiskey and their regular scotch, as well.

Their regular scotch was in a black ceramic bottle and the Suntory Royal was in a square shaped bottle with a top made to look like a pagoda. That interested the consumers and the liquor retailers, just to have on their shelves, as a conversation piece. In Japan, Suntory is a giant company. At the time they hired us, they were a billion dollar company producing over 100 products and had10,000 bars that they owned and operated, which was a complete source of sales for their own liquor products. They wanted to impress the Japanese consumers to see how popular and great they were in the world market. One of our projects was to send them all forms of publicity results with photos, videos and reprints of stories that they could show to their company executives in Japan, indicating they were so popular, that Americans were purchasing Suntory whiskey. In order to do that, we had a very aggressive contact program for the liquor stores and the bars. For image, we made contacts with the movie industry for product placement in their movies, so we could actually be part of movie scenes where whiskey was being used.

The publicity community for the movie industry was very aware of our program. In fact, we distributed small ceramic sample bottles of Suntory Royal at many of the industry's events.

One day, we were called by a movie promoter telling us he had a tremendous opportunity for Suntory to get exposure in a new movie. He said he would like to present it to us personally. We agreed that he could come to our office. He must have been very desperate because most movie promoters would be very independent and would have us come to them. He came to the office and told us that they were producing a movie called "Rocky." They expected this to be a major success because it was a good old-fashion story about an underdog becoming a champion. He wanted money to help him finish producing the movie. He actually told us that they were short of funds and needed extra money for the big scene at the end of the movie. He gave us the script and pointed out certain parts that would interest us. Mainly, that Rocky (Sylvester Stalone) was a young boxer who managed to fight his way up and have a chance to fight the champion. This was going to take place in Philadelphia. In the scene, Rocky wore a boxer's robe and on the back of the robe, the promoter suggested that we could put the name, Suntory Whiskey.

Millions of people would see it. Guess what? He asked for a $50,000 fee. Wow! That was more than a few years of budget for us from that account. We told him that we could not handle it. He immediately started coming down on the price, so we knew he was desperate. We also told him that it would not make sense that Suntory Whiskey, from Japan, was in a boxing scene in Philadelphia.

However, one of our other client's products we were promoting at that time was Binaca, breath freshener. Their theme was "Have a binaca blast." We told the promoter we would call this client and see if he could come up with some money and, believe it or not, at that time the promoter lowered the price all the way down to $5,000. We called the Binaca marketing director and told him about the movie and the script. He told us that he was sorry that he was out of budget. He said it sounded like a good idea, but that they could not cover it. We pleaded with him because we thought it would be a tremendous opportunity. A lot of people would see the logo because it would be on the back of the boxer's robe. In fact, we told him that we could cancel some of the game shows (The Price is Right, Wheel of Fortune and Let's Make a Deal) on which we were currently promoting the "Binaca blast." We suggested using just a couple of the promotional fees to get some money to appear in the movie. He told us he could not do that because he had already begun a big promotion to the retailers, bragging about the game shows. Well, that was bust. We still thought it was a good idea. Of course the promoter kept after us.

We immediately called the vice president of public relations at Frito Lay, which we also represented and told him about this great movie placement opportunity. He was very savvy and said it sounded like a very good opportunity. Unfortunately, his public relations budget was already committed.

The next day, the movie promoter called me and said he had an idea. They needed a big audience for their boxing match scene. They did not have enough budget for them to pay extras from the movie industry to be in the audience, watching the boxing match. So, he made a deal with KHJ Radio in Los Angeles, to announce he needed an audience at a big event that would be happening the next day. If any of the stations listeners wanted to be in a movie they should show up at 9AM the next day at the sports arena. The station promoted the event all day and encouraged people to come watch a boxing match and be in the audience for the movie scene. In order to make it more appealing they would give the audience drinks and snacks to eat. They also made a deal with Coca Cola for free soda.

So, here is where the adventure made many twists and turns, having started with Suntory and then going to Binaca and Fritos and being turned down. We suggested that we could help the movie production company with the free food. We told him if we got some exposure in exchange, somehow or other, we would give him a large supply of hard boiled eggs and Fritos. He grabbed the opportunity. The reason for eggs was, because in the script, there was a scene where Rocky would gulp down a big jug of raw eggs to give him strength. Since we handled the California egg producers, we would certainly impress them, showing that there was a message in the movie that eggs were nutritious and healthy. We negotiated with the promoter who put a small Fritos sign over the entrance to the arena that would be scene in the film for a few seconds. This was going to be exciting.

My two sons and I drove down the next day with a station wagon full of the eggs and Fritos and delivered it to the sports arena and watched the scenes, noting the audience eating eggs and bags of Fritos. We took many photos to use for future publicity in connection with the release of the film. The movie promoter was thrilled that a few hundred people who heard the radio announcement actually showed up.

As you know, "Rocky" was a huge success. We received exposure for two of our clients, eggs and Fritos. I never called the two clients, I originally contacted, to "rub it in" about the robe and all the exposure they would have received. Incidentally, in the movie, they ended up putting the name of Rocky's brother-in-law's meat packing company on the back of the robe that Rocky wore. What a missed opportunity, especially since "Rocky" had since been on TV several times, for even greater exposure, for just $5,000.

We learned something that I then used throughout the rest of my PR career. Most clients make a budget and when it is spent, they cannot take advantage of any unforeseen opportunities. As part of our working operation and advising our clients on their budgets from that time on, we would always tell them you never know when an opportunity will come up that could be very rewarding. If the opportunity does not come up, you do not spend that part of the budget, if it does, you can use your judgment and take advantage of it. This was a good example and we now always ask our clients to set up a "budget reserve." This was certainly a "rocky adventure."

Chapter 26

FRITOS HAS METAL CHIPS

One evening, on the local Los Angeles CBS Television station, I saw a shocker while watching the news. The consumer reporter speaking from her desk said, "Tonight I have a special story that just happened here, at the station." Then, she held up a bag of Fritos and reported that she just purchased that bag in the station's commissary vending machine just before going on the air. She explained that when she opened the bag up, in addition to the corn chips she also found little chips of metal and showed them in her hand, as the camera shot a close up. She said, "This must be a new product that Fritos just came out with," facetiously of course. Then she talked about the problems of finding things in snack bags and how bad it was. Everything went downhill from there. Well, what do you do when this happens? She was talking about our big account, Frito Lay. This was the beginning of a crisis public relations situation.

We called up our client in Dallas at home because of the time difference. He would set things in motion. Early the next morning, we called the plant manager in Los Angeles and he had already been alerted by headquarters. Fortunately, they have a great system of quality control and he immediately investigated what was wrong and discovered that the bag in question was found in Hollywood and that it was a small snack pack in a vending machine. Not the larger bag size found in supermarkets.

They knew exactly which area of the machinery in the plant that the product was packaged on. The manager and his crew immediately inspected the entire belt line and they found that one of the metal bands had worn out, and a few metal chips obviously mixed in with the Frito chips on the assembly line. At least he knew right away where and why it happened. He also knew exactly how many packages were produced and to what specific areas they were sent, because as part of their quality control every bag is coded and he could see exactly what vending machines in what buildings received this batch of product.

The CBS-TV commissary was obviously one of these locations. There were several other buildings in Hollywood that also received these bags, but fortunately none of them had any metal chips in them. Immediately, they alerted their drivers to go out the next morning, very early and pick up all of the products that were at CBS and in the other neighborhood vending machines.

We called up CBS TV news and spoke personally with the consumer reporter and told her that we discovered exactly what happened which created her news story the previous night about Fritos. We asked her if she could bring a camera crew out to the Frito Lay plant, and have them see "exactly" what happened and how the bags were inspected and why the metal chips ended up in the bag in the first place, and what was done about it.

She came out that afternoon with a camera crew and the plant manager showed her exactly how they package the Fritos, how they are inspected and exactly how this incidence happened, and why it will not happen again. The plant manager showed her how they produce millions of packages and how they have a quality control system in place. They, of course, were very sorry this occurred. He showed her how they immediately followed up and recalled all of the suspect packages. And that it so happens that there were only three packages with little metal chips in them and they all ended up in her station's vending machine. No other packages were found to contain metal chips in any other vending machines in Hollywood.

She was very impressed with what she heard and what she saw, especially how careful they followed through with everything and she liked their quality control system and how all the bags were coded and they literally knew where every one of their bags was delivered. She shot video of the assembly line and showed exactly what happened and why it won't happen again, due to their constant inspections.

That night, she gave a new report of the "metal chips in Fritos" story. She explained how she personally investigated this situation at the Frito Lay plant and was impressed with Frito Lay's quality control inspections, and this incident was just an anomaly.

This just happens one in a million times. And actually, the reporter was very complimentary to Frito-Lay as a company with great quality control. So, what started out as a liability, a true crisis situation, turned out to be a positive story about our client. In fact, it was a lucky break for Fritos, and also a lucky break that it was only on the local news so it never went national.

It would have been a disaster if it was picked up nationally and it could have been a disaster if we didn't invite the reporter to our client's plant. So, all's well that ends well and of course, we learned when a crisis happens, you have to stop everything and cover it immediately. This was a perfect example of how to handle a crisis. So, this was quite an adventure, and a bonus was we turned some negative publicity to a good deal of positive publicity.

Chapter 27

NIXON'S NUTRITION CONFERENCE

The California Dairy Council retained Lee & Associates to promote milk and eggs. Back then, from 1956 through 1992, we had the USDA's Basic Four Food Groups, which were Milk, Vegetables and Fruit, Cereal and Bread, and Meat, which included eggs. Our job was to support the 21 dietitians who traveled throughout the state lecturing at schools and special events. We helped them encourage people to consume dairy products as part of the USDA Four Food Groups nutritional promotion.

We developed several television public service announcements (PSAs) for the California Dairy Council. They promoted eating a big breakfast and eating healthier foods along with diary products. The public reacted positively to these PSAs, which featured celebrities and sports figures.

President Nixon held the first Nutrition Conference in Washington, D.C., in December, 1969. Its purpose was to obtain recommendations from experts on how to end hunger and malnutrition among the poor in the United States. Dr. Gene Mayer, Director of Harvard's

Nutrition Department, was chosen to create and manage the conference. He invited scientists, doctors, nutritionists, food experts and representatives from related fields to convene for this landmark conference. The problems of poverty, malnutrition, junk foods and lack of exercise discussed then are even more relevant today.

The USDA knew of Lee & Associates' public relations program for the California Dairy Council and wanted me to share my knowledge at the conference about what we were doing and how we were doing it. I was thrilled at the recognition and the invitation to attend, and excited to go to Washington, D.C. as a panel participant.

Doctor Phillip White was the President of the American Medical Association and I was honored to be on his panel, which was tasked with how to reach the disadvantaged with proper nutrition education. We identified the core problem: while the government's campaign proseletized the Four Food Groups via all manner of printed stories and releases, that information was not reaching the intended audience. Those most in need were not reading or following up with the information.

"You don't reach the disadvantaged by newspaper," I told the panel. "You can't reach them with just facts or recommendations. You capture their attention and reach them through the people they respect and emulate, like sports celebrities and actors that they recognize from radio, TV or the movies."

I told the panel about the "Julia" show, for example, which was a popular TV show produced by 20th Century Fox. In it, Diane Carol, a very talented actress, portrayed a single African-American mother with a young son, and the activities and life of this mother and son were humorously and poignantly showcased. I related to the panel how my agency worked with 20th Century on behalf of the California

Dairy Council and convinced the writers to put a scene in the script showing the son coming home from school and his mother giving him a glass of milk and a cookie to keep him from having a soda pop or other sweet drinks. This was a win-win for the Dairy Council and 20th Century Studios, as it was effective in promoting dairy products and good for the show's ratings.

As I finished telling that story, I threw in a reference to the success of the "big breakfast" milk and egg public service announcements that featured well-known athletes and actors. A panel member who was a disc jockey in Chicago, a rebel type, who complained about everything wrong with the government and with society, jumped up, saying, "Well, you rich guys can have a big breakfast, but our kids are too poor to have a big breakfast so we give them Twinkies and Kool Aid for breakfast to get them off." Wow! That was a shocker. He went on and on about the problems in Chicago. Because of him, the press captured our panel with the headline, "Twinkies and Kool-Aid For Breakfast." While it was certainly a catchy headline with the wrong message, the story actually presented all of our information and covered all of our important points.

The conference had many successful outcomes in reducing hunger and malnutrition through improved child nutrition programs and consumer education and outreach.

That was over 40 years ago. Fast forward and nutrition is at the forefront of our country's renewed focus on health and well-being, with plenty of celebrity M.D.s, Ph.D.s, and self-proclaimed food experts, giving us advice on buying, preparing, and eating food to stay healthy and fit. There is only one thing around in a big way today that was not here 40 years ago, and that is obesity. The United States has put on weight over the last 40 years! Even First Lady Michelle

Obama created her "Let's Move" program to encourage kids' healthy food habits and physical activities to reduce rates of obesity.

So, sometimes it takes much more time than expected. But I'm happy my very exciting adventure with nutrition and the Nixon administration some 40 years ago helped pave the way for today's nutritional awareness.

Chapter 28

"IN LIKE FLINT" MOVIE HEALTH BAR

This is what I would call a fun, healthy adventure. One day, when we were preparing for an appearance at a trade show and we needed an attractive spokesperson to help us at the exhibit, we called one of our favorite actress/models to hire her. She told us that she could not make it because she just got a job to appear in a movie at 20th Century Fox. We knew how important that was for her and congratulated her on her part and told her we would call her again for another spokesperson job after the movie was completed. We then called another one of our spokesperson and she also told us she was in a movie at 20th Century Fox and would no be available. Believe it or not, a third spokesperson we called also told us the same thing. She mentioned that the name of the movie was "In Like Flint." The movie starred James Coburn who, at that time, was a very popular actor. This peaked our interest.

We called the 20th Century Fox public relations executive, with whom we worked before, and told him the coincidence that three of our spokespersons were in that movie. We asked if he could tell us about it and maybe there was some way we could tie in with it. The movie was about a group of very beautiful, strong "amazons" who were masquerading as operators at a beauty spa on a remote island who were ready to conquer the world. There would be lots of action and beautiful women. A great combination.

We discussed what could we do with our "healthy foods" clients to tie in with these beautiful, healthy and strong women. After much discussion, we came up with an idea that was a winner. It was very simple and something actually newsworthy. Most studios that were making a movie would have a coffee bar on the set for the crew and actors and would have coffee and doughnuts and other sweets. We decided that since we had clients that had products that were "healthy," we could offer them a "health bar" instead, to tie in with their theme of healthy, strong amazon women. So, they made a big sign that read "In Like Flint Health Bar," which included boysenberries, apples, Danish cheese, Altadena milk, hard-boiled eggs and apple juice, all clients of ours. This was certainly quite different from what was usually on a movie set.

"In Like Flint" sports Hollywood's first on-set healthy juice bar.

The entertainment media reporters who were doing stories on the background of filming the movie were curious and impressed with this health bar. They showed up to take photos of all of these beautiful women. These young ladies were dressed in their amazon costumes, eating and drinking healthy foods and juices. We also took our own photos, too, and sent them to the grocery trade publications, showing the grocers we were promoting this movie with these healthy products, which also impressed them. Frankly, it was a win-win situation for us because we did not have to pay for the models, in this case. Upon the completion, the movie was a huge success.

I would call it a "healthy" adventure. The studio was pleased and all our client's were happy as well.

Chapter 29

SEAN PENN HATES CROUTONS

Here is an adventure that is a promotion person's dream. We all dream if something were to happen in the media in the newspaper or on radio or TV, where someone else says something nice about our client's product, not a commercial, but rather, part of programming. I'd like to share one such an amazing experience with you. Here is how this adventure happened.

One day, my son, Frank, was driving home from work listening to the Larry Elder show on KABC Talk Radio, in Los Angeles. Larry Elder always looked for controversy. He was a popular host who talked about stories that were provocative. He had mentioned several times that he did not like the actor, Sean Penn, as they disagreed on several political issues.

Larry told his listeners, one day, that he read an article in the Los Angeles Times, which said that Sean Penn did not like croutons on his salad. Larry said, "Finally, I agree with Sean on something, because I don't like croutons on my salad either." Then, Larry went ahead with a long discussion about how he never tasted a crouton that had enough crunch or flavor. He talked about his dislike for croutons as much as he would any of the serious political or controversial subjects on his show.

Frank immediately called me and my other son, Howard, and told us what he had heard while driving home. This is prime time and there were many people listening. Since we represented Mrs. Cubbison's Croutons, we were certainly concerned and wanted to do something positive about this. Howard called the president of Mrs. Cubbison's and told him what had happened. We all decided to do something quickly, so we could get some positive publicity about croutons on Larry's show by the next day.

We decided that we would write a letter from Ron Parque, Mrs. Cubbison's president. But, not a letter complaining, rather a friendly, funny letter, telling Larry that perhaps he did not like croutons because he had not tasted the "right" croutons and we would like him to try the Mrs. Cubbison's Croutons we were sending over with the letter.

However, there was a big problem. This incident occurred right after the 9/11 tragedy. We knew that there would be a high level of security at the radio station, which would certainly not accept the delivery of a package that may have looked suspicious. Since we could not just have a case of croutons delivered to Larry, Howard called his sales representative at the station, with whom he had worked many times for various promotions. Howard asked him if he would please help us and deliver a box with several packages of Mrs. Cubbison's Croutons to Larry's desk with the letter from the company's president, so Larry would see it just prior to going on the air the next day.

The sales rep told Howard, of course he would be happy to help us as not only were we advertisers on the station, but also this sounded like a fun topic for Larry to discuss on his normally serious show.

The next day, just prior to starting his show, Larry opened up the box with the various flavors of croutons inside and read the letter and liked the idea of discussing this subject, especially after he finally agreed with Sean Penn about disliking croutons. He was now ready to be convinced otherwise, so once again, he would be in disagreement with him. Much to our delight, he read Ron's letter on the air and said he tried a few flavors of the Mrs. Cubbison's Croutons, just moments before going on the air. In fact, he said, "These taste great!" After reading Ron's letter on the air and describing how delicious, crunchy, and tasty Mrs. Cubbison's Croutons were, Larry kidded about it throughout his entire show, netting more than several minutes of on-air plugs for our client.

Not only that, but at the end of his show he started talking with Ira Mandell, who hosted the next show, about the croutons and offered him a taste of a few of the different flavors he had received. Ira also said, "These do taste great and I wish they would've sent me some, as well." So, of course, we had a case of Mrs. Cubbison's Croutons delivered to Ira the next day at the station, again with the help of our radio representative. And, believe it or not, the next day, when Larry and Ira were talking on-air between their two shows, Ira told Larry that he was happy to receive his own personal samples of Mrs. Cubbison's Croutons, too. Now we were receiving even more positive publicity on KABC Talk Radio.

Who could believe, that by just hearing a mention about a client, could spark all of this great, fun, positive publicity? We were able to get a tape of all of these mentions about Mrs. Cubbison's Croutons from our representative at the station and we made copies of this tremendous publicity event and sent them out to the major supermarket retailers, sharing this great exposure of our client's product. This was one great adventure that would not have happened if we did not follow up on this opportunity immediately. It reinforced our agency's policy of keeping our eyes and ears open for any opportunity and reacting immediately.

Chapter 30

SOCIAL MEDIA - THE GOOD AND THE BAD

We all know how powerful social media is as a direct means of communication. In addition to all of the personal stories and photos that are so popular on Facebook, the commercial companies have made strides in using this form of reaching consumers to promote their products. This adventure is one where a commercial company included the messages that backfired and actually caused a disastrous complete contradiction to what they were promoting. In order to fully understand how it happened, let me give you the background.

We handled the advertising and public relations for Mrs. Cubbison's Foods. We were promoting Mrs. Cubbison's Prepared Dressing for poultry, meat and fish (some people called it stuffing mix). The whole idea was to show customers that they could prepare the stuffing with their Thanksgiving and Christmas turkey, just like grandma did, without all of the work. The product was already prepared with toasted bread and was seasoned just right. All the cook had to do was add their favorite ingredients without the necessity of finding a variety of correct spices and chopping up stale bread. This product grew in popularity. All we had to do was provide a variety of traditional and contemporary recipes. We would remind the old cooks and teach the new cooks. It was a very rewarding and interesting promotion.

Most of the promotion took place starting three weeks before Thanksgiving. We had a reasonable budget that allowed us to purchase radio commercials in the eleven Western states and to have a very aggressive public relations program where we sent food photos and recipes to the newspapers. And, our spokespersons appeared on radio and television with handy cooking hints for the holiday. In order to be accepted by the media, we provided interesting facts and recipes for the turkey and the trimmings. Now, here is where we get ready for the adventure.

In our commercials and publicity appearances, we said these handy hints and other recipes for your holiday dinner are available at www.thanksgivingtips.com. That was a domain name we created to be attached to www.mrscubbisons.com. This worked fantastically for many years. After having this account for 62 years, the company was sold and we discovered soon that the new owners had their own staff doing many of the things that we did. For example, they had a staff chef, artist and social media director. So, they directed us not to pursue those duties and let us do our basic advertising and publicity. We still recommended that the consumers visit our website, but were no longer in control of the content.

We started our program and had many TV and radio interviews and commercials, mostly two weeks before the shopping days for Thanksgiving. Our home economist spokesperson decided to see what kind of contemporary recipes the company chef came up with and when she looked at them online, she was horrified. She called us immediately. The chef, with great fanfare, listed the first five of his recipes with instructions that called for cooking from scratch and using stale bread, cornbread and several spices which was completely contrary to the Mrs.Cubbison's product itself. We were completely shocked. Here, on social media, Mrs. Cubbison's is actually telling her customers "not to buy" her product. We immediately called the marketing director. It is hard to believe that he did not know about it. He immediately had those recipes deleted. We did not know how many people had already seen it, but based on past experience we knew that it must have been a tremendous number. We hoped we saved the day for the company, saving the rest of the content for the large number of remaining consumers before the holiday.

I am sure you will agree that this is one for the books that should not have happened. It certainly illustrates the "bad" that could happen, due to carelessness by the provider of content.

Chapter 31

MUSTARD AND BASKETBALL

Mustard and basketball. That sure is a strange combination. Let me give you the background and share this adventure with you. One of our clients was Morehouse Mustard, a fourth generation family company, based in Los Angeles. They manufactured mustard that was sold internationally and was known as a private label for several companies. Their own brand, Morehouse, was the most popular mustard in California and adjacent states.

They had just recently celebrated their hundredth anniversary. We were fortunate to get a tremendous interest from the press with many stories about the history of the company with photos going back to the early 1900s. Dave Latter, the CEO, loved to talk about mustard and appeared on many radio and TV shows that we arranged. We had placed many stories in the consumer and grocery press with his interviews.

Now here comes the connection. My son Frank, who worked on this account with his brother, Howard, and me, is an avid sports fan. One day, he came in and told us that Chick Hearn, the famous

Lakers basketball sports announcer, was going to celebrate his three thousand consecutive "live" broadcast in a couple of days. All of the fans always enjoyed the game immensely, with his professional and humorous calls on all of the plays. Chick was famous for his "Chickisms." He had descriptive words and sayings for every description of what was going on during the game, such as "Slam-dunk," "No harm, no foul," "This game's in the refrigerator" (meaning the game's outcome is already set), "He's in the popcorn machine" (when a defending player got faked in the air by a fake pump), to name a few. But, his most popular Chickism was when a hotshot, show-off player would take a fancy shot and miss. He would say "The mustard's off the hot dog." Everybody knew exactly what happened.

So, here is how everything came together. We had a mustard client and the Lakers basketball team had Chick Hearn and his Chickisms. We got our staff together and started sharing ideas. What could we do to take advantage of this major event, because the 3000th broadcast was going to be big news. So, we decided to create a beautiful plaque honoring Chick Hearn, thanking him for his many great broadcasts and also mention Morehouse Mustard was celebrating their hundredth anniversary, two great events. We also added to the plaque his popular saying, "The mustard's off the hot dog."

Howard then contacted the publicist at the Los Angeles Lakers headquarters and told him about our idea of presenting a plaque to Chick and, believe it or not, they jumped at it. Well, why not? It is good publicity and goodwill for both parties. The publicist told Howard that we could come out on Media Day and honor Chick and be part of all of the media activities. Sometime during that day, we would be given a time slot for taking photos while presenting Chick with our plaque.

So, we went ahead and produced the plaque, honoring him and thanking him, of course, on behalf of Morehouse Mustard, celebrating their hundredth anniversary. Howard and Frank met Dave on Media day at The Forum and Howard brought some props with them. He brought, of course, a couple of bottles of Morehouse Mustard, some hot dogs on a bun and the plaque. They were patiently waiting for their time to take photos. You can imagine all of the heavyweight, big-shot sports writers and broadcasters who were there, as well.

Prior to their time slot for the photo session with Chick, CNN TV had just finished taping its national TV interview. We were next. Howard went over to the newscaster from CNN and told him about our plaque and said this might be a good add-on to their interview, because of the great visual with the mustard and hot dog props. They, of course, knew about Chick's "The mustard's off the hot dog" Chickism. Chick and our mustard client began talking. Being very gracious and having a good sense of humor, Chick took a hot dog on a bun and started pouring the mustard on it and a lot of photographers were taking tons of pictures. The camera man from CNN got the whole thing on tape, even showing all the photographers taking many photos. This was fantastic for our client. When the Chick Hearn story aired on CNN, our part of the segment ran at the end of the story, as the reporter commented, "Chick Hearn put the mustard 'back' on the hot dog, helping to celebrate Morehouse Mustard's hundredth anniversary."

Our client received a great deal of local and national exposure from this plaque presentation that we created. The next day, we sent out our own release to sports writers, broadcasters and the grocery industry media, telling all about this historic event. There was no social media at that time. But, I can assure you if there was, this would have gone viral. It basically did, however, with the existing media, as we picked up stories with photos in newspapers all over the country, plus exposure on local and national TV because of our CNN story. Dave Latter, Morehouse's CEO received dozens of phone calls from many friends and customers from around the country, telling him that they either heard or saw stories about his hundredth anniversary, related to the Chick Hearn event. This sports connection was certainly strange, but definitely a huge success and quite a fun adventure.

Chapter 32

THE PIZZA BOWL COOK OFF

ere is an adventure that, for us, was enjoyable, interesting and very exciting. This promotion not only involved public relations activities, but it was almost like putting on a big, theatrical show. Our entire staff was involved.

It all began when the manufacturers of the very popular Chef Boyardee food products company retained us for a specific marketing project. They created a massive advertising campaign to promote the Chef Boyardee "Pizza Bowl Cook Off." This was fashioned after the famous Pillsbury Cook Off, with a totally different approach using the Super Bowl theme. They advertised to cooks all over the country through women's magazines, encouraging them to enter a cooking contest with their favorite recipe, using Chef Boyardee's pizza mix. The consumers were to purchase the pizza mix and prepare their favorite recipe and submit it to the company and write down their favorite NFL team on the outside of the envelop. One finalist representing each of the 32 football teams who was judged to have the best recipe from that group would compete for many valuable prizes. These included cash and food products and home appliances. Prestigious, professional cooking judges would take care of the preliminary judging.

In the final stage of the event, the judges were all prominent figures in the food and entertainment industries. The event was held at the Hyatt Regency Hotel in Los Angeles. Our job was two-fold. Number one, we were to publicize this event before, during and after. Number two, we were to work with the client's team who handled all of the arrangements to put on the event. There was another very important ingredient. To keep within Super Bowl theme, they hired two-time Super Bowl winner Joe Theismann, the quarterback of the Washington Redskins. He was the spokesperson for the event and, obviously would be a reason for the entire sports media and consumer press to attend.

Here are just a few of the advance arrangements. We had to coordinate with the hotel staff and arrange for two giant ballrooms, one for the cooking event, which would include an individual stove and work station for each contestant, as well as a room for proper facilities for the press, the clients and the main judges for tasting. We also made arrangements for purchasing the food supplies, made arrangements for the presentation and final judging, in addition to arranging entertainment for the audience while waiting for the results, plus all sorts of logistics had to be handled.

On the public relations side, it was a dream. We were to promote appearances on radio and television and in newspapers for sports stories, food stories and also trade stories for the grocers. One massive chore was that we had to have all of the semi-finalists' recipes totally prepared for release as soon as the winners would be announced. At the same time, we were in contact with the major supermarket retailers who would make displays for Chef Boyardee with sales material provided by our client and could also, in their own media outlets, feature the winners' recipes, which naturally, could encourage the sales of the many other various ingredients used in the recipes. Frankly, it was like an army maneuver.

My son, Frank, who is an avid sports fan, was thrilled to spend the day with Joe Theisman, driving him to many TV and radio interviews. Joe was a captive audience for big sports fan, Frank, who must have asked him a million football questions while going to the various stations throughout Los Angeles. I, personally, having grown up in the food business, loved working with our staff, shopping at the market for all the recipe ingredients and paying a gigantic food tab (with the client's money) when they completed their shopping. Incidentally, we took many photos that certainly added to our publicity kit. It was also rewarding to arrange to have the Mayor proclaim "National Pizza Week" in Los Angeles. We also served pizza to the city council members the day before the event, getting even more publicity attention in the news. Another pleasant chore was to invite many highly-visible members of the entertainment, sports and food industries, as well as civic leaders, to attend and watch the judging.

The final event had lots of fanfare and here is where we had to make some adjustments and finish up as a huge success. The winner was chosen. She was a very accomplished cook but, was extremely shy. We immediately noticed that she had trouble relating her thrill of being chosen to the press. They threw a million questions at her and practically frightened her to death. She was just a regular homemaker, operating a beauty store and now, suddenly thrown into the limelight.

We immediately put Joe Theismann on stage and let him do all the talking to the press.

All is well that ends well. It was a great adventure and a total reward for all of us, with lots of local and national publicity for Chef Boyardee's "Pizza Bowl Cook Off."

Chapter 33

GASTROENTEROLOGISTS CONVENTION WITH A TROUBLED BEGINNING

This adventure is one where we survived, despite two major problems that occurred. One where the TV reporters did not show up as promised and, the other was a very unethical act by a PR agency.

We were retained by the American Gastroenterological Association to handle the public relations for their annual three-day meeting, being held at the Disneyland Hotel in Anaheim. We were to do the normal public relations of reporting news about the speeches, new information and new medical devices. But this particular year, we were instructed to report on education, as well, and get as much information out about the field of gastroenterology as possible. They were concerned that the government and the business community in general, as well as consumers, did not have as much interest or knowledge in their particular specialty, as compared to cancer, heart, kidney, lungs and all of the other diseases that were getting grants for research. Their particular specialty needed research, too.

We, ourselves, soon learned that these physicians were concerned with the stomach, esophagus, small intestine, large intestine and biliary system (liver, pancreas, gallbladder and bile ducts). These all certainly needed research to find cures. We set up the preliminary contacts, especially with the local television stations. We advised them in advance about some of the speeches and activities that would be taking place with this specialty field, at the event.

I assigned my son, Frank, to handle the press room at the association's annual meeting. My other son, Howard, and I would stay in Los Angeles and would handle things by phone. Frank drove down to Anaheim. He called up and said, "None of the television stations have shown up." Well, that's strange. We were in touch with the news directors. They all indicated their interest. Howard called some of the stations and found out that Betty Ford, President Gerald Ford's wife, signed herself into the Long Beach Naval Hospital to be treated for alcoholism. It was a huge news story. This was the first time, a prominent person especially the wife of a president, told the world about her personal alcohol problem. Obviously, it was tremendous news. All the television stations came down to Long Beach to cover that story. We certainly understood.

About an hour later, Frank called again and said that something totally strange happened. One of the most important speeches that was going to be held the next day was by a medical professor of Columbia University, in New York, who did a study about how acetaminophen (Tylenol was the main brand) mixed with alcohol resulted in many liver failures and death. He was going to present the entire story about the study. Not only was acetaminophen involved with overdosing for children and in general, it also included the fact that in England, people who wanted to commit suicide would overdose with acetaminophen. Naturally, that was a huge subject. Tylenol's medical director was attending the convention to rebut the story. The makers of Bayer aspirin were, of course, delighted. The conclusion of the presentation would recommend that Tylenol and other manufacturers of acetaminophen should include special warnings on their labels.

Frank called us and said that while he was talking to a reporter, a woman was browsing through the press room and she picked up the entire stack of releases about the acetaminophen report. Then she walked out of the room. He could not follow her to see what she was doing, as he was in the middle of an interview. He called us about this strange occurrence. What could that be? We knew the giant Los Angeles PR agency that represented Tylenol and we thought they were the only ones who could benefit from taking this big stack of releases.

I called the head of the office and told him what happened and busted his agency. I told him that it must have been someone from his office and said it was totally unethical. I told him that I was going to report this incident to the Public Relations Society of America and the press. He was flabbergasted. He said that his office was not involved and found out the main agency in New York had sent out their own people to cover the convention. He promised he would follow through immediately and asked us not to do anything yet, and that he was an honorable practitioner and would never do such a thing. Whoever did it, from the New York office, should be accountable. He said he would call us back immediately, which he did, and told us that there was a young women who was assigned to come out with the medical director and that they were concerned with this particular story about acetaminophen that was going to take place tomorrow.

We told him that we were going to reprint our releases and the least he could do was pay for it. He certainly agreed. Frankly, he was very frightened that we would make a big fuss about it. So, Frank arranged to reprint the releases at the hotel. Fortunately, he had the original copies in his own press book.

The next day was the big presentation of the report on acetaminophen. We expected the Los Angeles TV stations to cover it. Again, they did not show up. We found out that the police finally arrested the two murderers called the Hillside Stranglers who had killed 10 females and were being hunted for four months. That was the hottest news of the day and naturally our story could not compete with that.

The convention proceeded, speeches were made and everything worked out all right. Once again, you never know what can happen with things over which you have no control. It is interesting to note, Betty Ford helped start an alcohol rehabilitation treatment, which is called the Betty Ford Center in Rancho Mirage, CA.

The FDA started proceedings to change the labels of acetaminophen and, after many years of legal delays, finally in 2009, the FDA required the changes in the labels. Tylenol included these words on the cap, "Contains acetaminophen. Always read the label." On the label it says, "Do not drink alcoholic beverages and do not overdose."

That adventure had many twists and turns. But we came out on top and the American Gastroenterological Association received plenty of positive publicity for their worthwhile activities.

Chapter 34

DAVID AND GOLIATH, A FOOD BATTLE

Here is an adventure that resembled the David and Goliath story. We were handling the public relations and advertising for a company from Canada called Woodstone Foods. This was a very interesting account. Pea fiber was a powder with no odor or taste and could be used as an important ingredient to make a lot of foods healthier. They sold their product to manufacturers who used it in their processing for baked, canned, frozen and refrigerated foods to help the formula and also show healthy items on their label. This pea fiber could be used in the manufacturing of ice cream, pizza dough, bread, various frozen foods and just about anything else. One problem Woodstone had was they were competing with the giant companies who had similar products. In business, buyers always seem to gravitate towards the big companies. Small companies have a job of convincing them they have product and service that would also be a benefit. Woodstone's main goal was to reach the food technologists and the marketers of the wide variety of food products and show them the value and ease of use and advantages of their pea fiber.

One of the best sources for food sales departments making presentations to the buyers for manufacturers was the annual IFT convention (International Food Technologists). This convention was held in New Orleans that year. It was attended by practically every food manufacturer from not only throughout the country, but from the rest of the world. All of the suppliers would have exhibits to "show and tell" their products, and of course, sample them. And they had a food technologist to answer questions. It was normal, from a marketing point of view, that the big companies would put on large, special invitational parties in their suites at a big hotel where they would entertain and talk business, trying to set the stage for final sales.

Our little client wanted to compete on the same level and told us to create a hospitality room and do all the things that could encourage attendance and make a "big impression." We planned a party in our client's suite. But, how could we be different? Our client provided us with a list of all of their customers and potential customers. We brainstormed for quite a while. What could we do? We came up with several ideas and put them to work. Since it was in New Orleans, we decided to have a theme "New Orleans food and fun." New Orleans was famous for its food, music and upscale restaurants.

We hired a top chef from one of the most popular restaurants to prepare New Orleans foods and several of our own food items to be presented in our suite, as well as, to the guests, which allowed us to talk about and describe the dishes with our client's pea fiber. Then, we hired a local convention party planning company and they helped us come up with the New Orleans theme. They supplied us with neon signs, imitation palm trees, a bourbon street sign and we decorated our suite inside and outside replicating New Orleans. Then we also hired one of the top New Orleans musicians to play piano at our party. The next step was, we would come up with a clever invitation. Realizing that the other companies were sending out invitations, we had to do something different. We came up with the idea of sending an invitation listing some of the food items that we were going to serve and a musical and verbal cassette in a very attractive small black and gold box. In those days, practically everyone's car had a cassette player and we thought, out of curiosity, the invitees would play the cassettes while they were driving.

One of our staff members had a beautiful, deep voice, perfect for recording. So, we used him to narrate a special tape we made. Here is what we did. We started the cassette with some cool, New Orleans jazz to get their attention. Then, in his fantastic announcer voice, he said, "I'm your Woodstone Maitre d' and I'm inviting you to attend a fantastic party featuring delicious New Orleans food, live jazz music and lots of fun. You'll meet a top New Orleans chef and taste his famous dishes, as well as, samples of how many of your own products could be improved with health and nutrition, using Woodstone pea fiber. We are looking forward to greeting you. Enjoy the rest of this cassette with some enjoyable New Orleans jazz."

We were certainly a bit nervous about how many people might show up when we were competing against so many other huge, expensive parties going on that night. As the evening progressed, more and more guests showed up and stayed for quite a while at our party, listening to our live jazz and more importantly, sampling all of the large variety of foods featuring our client's pea fiber. Our party was a huge success.

The next day at the convention, everyone was talking about the fun they had at the Woodstone party and how the chef did a tremendous job showing off the tasty foods. That party actually put us into the big time. The convention itself, was a huge success and sales for our client's product increased tremendously.

We certainly played the part of David versus Goliath and the client was extremely pleased.

Chapter 35

NORTON SIMON AND OUR REWARD

This is a strange adventure that I doubt will happen again. Because of our immediate action and advice from a fellow PR friend, the project was a huge success. Before I get into this adventure, let me give you some background.

We, in the public relations field, like many of the other professions, have specialists. Just as in the medical profession, where there is a specialist for every part of the body, in the public relations profession, there are also specialists who have become so because they were in a particular field and became proficient in it and also because they are more involved with more accounts in that particular field. Even though they are general practitioners, they can also be "specialists" in the areas of entertainment, political, financial, charity/fundraising and many others. In our case, we are in the area of marketing promotion of products and services. Within that specialty, we grew and became very involved in the food industry.

There have been occasions when we would call in a free-lancer PR person who specializes in another field that we did not know as much about concerning the contacts or the everyday working, in that area. There were occasions that we would meet our peers who were also friendly competitors, at meetings for the Public Relations Society of America or the Public Relations Counselors Group, where we would discuss problems of the industry to improve our activities. From time to time, some of them would call us about food questions, while we would call some of them about other areas, such as financial questions or medical and other areas with which we were not as familiar.

This adventure is one that involved two different incidences where friends called friends for help. One day, I received a frantic call from an old client and friend that created a whirlwind of activities with a tremendous reward to both of us. At this time, we were handling the public relations for Frito-Lay, specializing in West Coast promotional activities. Occasionally, we would also get projects and assignments from PepsiCo, the parent company. That was quite rewarding, the fact that this giant corporation would have us do projects for them. Don Rosendale, Vice President of Public Relations, was our client contact. Don left PepsiCo and took a position with Norton Simon, a giant conglomerate. He became vice president of Public Relations for their division called Norton Simon Communications, which handled the coordination, marketing and promotional programs on behalf of their corporate headquarters. They owned Hunt Foods, Wesson Oil, Avis, Canada Dry and several other major companies. Occasionally, Don would call us and ask for information about contacts or activities pertaining to Southern California.

Here is where this adventure begins. One day, nine o' clock in the morning, I received a frantic call from Don. I could tell immediately that he was totally freaked out, as he told me he needed my help immediately. He told me that the day before, Norton Simon Financial

Division had a stockholders meeting in Fullerton, CA at Hunt Foods, not far from Los Angeles. They had a tremendous amount of news to be released to the press. They were talking about Hunt Foods, especially. They said how successful Hunt Foods and their other companies were. They raised the stock dividend and made an announcement that even though corporate headquarters was in New York, they were going to shine the spotlight on the West Coast and add more attention and spend more funds and promote the headquarters in the West, primarily Hunt Foods and Wesson Oil. This was a very big story.

Much to their shegrin, the next day, which was the day that Don called me, the Los Angeles Times only had a few lines in a small story, about the increased dividend and omitted most of the main story news. Don's boss, David Mahoney, CEO of the entire corporation, was furious. He had a reputation in the industry of being one tough guy and was known to fire executives when things went wrong. In fact, Don actually expected to be fired, even though he had a very large public relations agency, it was his responsibility to obtain the required results. Mahoney expected a large story in the paper and did not get one.

It is hard to know what happened. You cannot control the news. Perhaps the agency did not follow through, as they should have. There are many reasons why it did not happen. Of course, the agency and Don were blamed. Don said to me, he had to do something immediately. He said, "I need your help, Leo. Stop what you're doing. We've got to get a story in the Los Angeles Times."

We know that history proves it is hard to have a story repeated if the paper decided not to use it in the first place or did not make too big of a deal about it. Perhaps they may use it later. But David Mahoney wanted that story out right now. Don gave us some of the details of the story. We brainstormed to see what else we could do. We were not involved too much in financial public relations and even though we could address the financial editor, we did not have the personal contact, nor did we have the proper tools with which to work. So, we did what we needed to do. We called our friend, Marj Walker, who was much more active in financial public relations than we were and certainly worked with the Los Angeles Times on a regular basis. She was a top PR person and a good friend, too. Luckily, Marj was available and we told her our story. We asked her what could we do? She said, first of all, no matter what, you have to call your client back and find out if there is any other angle that was not mentioned in the previous day's story. She said we would have to have something new to talk about to make it newsworthy all over again and get it to the paper immediately. She said to call a particular reporter, with whom she worked from time to time, and said to mention her name and tell him about yesterday's news story and that you had another angle about Norton Simon. We thanked her and called Don back.

This is amazing. Don said that Mahoney was going to UCLA that very day at noon, along with Norton Simon to present the university a million dollar grant to help future business students. Boy, that was real news. We immediately called up the reporter and told him about the fact that this was going to take place at noon and they were going to make the presentation in person. The reporter accepted the idea and asked us where they were staying and said he would come by with a cameraman within the next half hour. They were staying at the Century Plaza Hotel. We immediately contacted Mahoney. He did not know who we were. We told him we worked with Don Rosendale and we had to have him interviewed before he left for UCLA. We explained that we personally arranged for another shot at a big story in the Los Angeles Times, on his behalf. We rushed over to the hotel to meet everyone. Mahoney really was a tough guy, but was gracious to us. We mentioned to them that when he was being interviewed by this new reporter, to bring up all of yesterday's information that did not make it into the story plus, mention the new story about the rather generous million dollar donation to UCLA. The reporter was very professional. He did a fantastic interview with Mahoney and the cameraman took several photos.

The next day, in the Los Angeles Time, not only did we get a few photos, including a large photo of Mahoney, the Norton Simon feature literally dominated the financial page. It was a fantastic story. We saved Don's neck and impressed Mahoney, who by the way, fired his New York PR agency which had nothing to do with Don or us. He then hired us to handle projects for his company from then on, out of Los Angeles, the way we did for PepsiCo and Frito-Lay. Don was our boss out of Mahoney's New York headquarters. All's well that ends well.

The moral of the story is if we had not called our friend, Marj, we probably would not have been successful by doing things immediately and following through with correct instructions that helped us end up with a terrific account. This account lasted for over ten years, until the company was eventually sold to another corporation that had its own in-house public relations agency.

That was one exciting adventure that took place at full speed and kept us on our toes the entire time.

www.ingramcontent.com/pod-product-compliance
Lightning Source LLC
Chambersburg PA
CBHW071814200526
45169CB00018B/262